GANG MEMBER
Another Side of Democracy

PERCY TWENTY-FIVE BROWN

Copyright © 2024 by Percy Twenty-Five Brown.

Library of Congress Control Number: 2009904251
ISBN: 979-8-89465-028-9 (sc)
ISBN: 979-8-89465-065-4 (hb)
ISBN: 979-8-89465-029-6 (e)

All rights reserved. No part of this publication may be reproduced, distributed, or transmitted in any form or by any means, including photocopying, recording, or other electronic or mechanical methods, without the prior written permission of the author, except in the case of brief quotations embodied in critical reviews and certain other noncommercial uses permitted by copyright law.

Printed in the United States of America.

Integrity Publishing
39343 Harbor Hills Blvd Lady Lake, FL 32159

www.integrity-publishing.com

This story is true. Some of the names have been substituted.
Percy Twenty-Five Brown

To RUBY
In Memory of Grand Master Sang Kyu Shim
In Memory of Vanessa Nathan

"For though a righteous man may fall seven times, he will get up." (Proverbs 24:16)

CONTENTS

Foreword..ix

Chapters

1 The Time is At Hand....................................1
2 The Coldest Days 21
3 A Real Black Mafia 51
4 The Hit...60
5 The Birth of Crack....................................94
6 The Black Knight.....................................105
7 The New Name For Niggers 122

FOREWORD

It was in 1977, when I was summoned to court for non-payment of child support. My accuser worked for the Detroit Police Department, so the Judge thought I was lying when I said that I had no knowledge of the child. The Judge had me incarcerated without a DNA test after I made a few angry remarks. I ended up losing my job of seven years for Chrysler Corporation. I could not resolve the situation because each attorney naturally thought that I was trying to avoid child support and refused the case.

I ran to Los Angeles to avoid going back to jail and ended up becoming homeless and sleeping in a park. I was rescued by the gang that controlled an area of Los Angeles called "The Jungle". I became a gang member and eventually came to be third in command.

It was over twenty years before I resolved the matter with the courts. I had moved back to the place of my birth in Montgomery Alabama. I had joined the Dexter Avenue King Memorial Baptist Church when one of the Deacons became interested in my story. "We can't help a lot of our young men today because we don't know the mindset of some of these gang members." From his statement, I was inspired to write about my gang experience. The story is true.

CHAPTER ONE

The Time is At Hand

"The time is at hand!" Kojac said, as he entered Omar's apartment. The apartment was located in an area of Los Angeles known as "The Jungle." It was a high crime area. "The Jungle" was a good indication of what the place was like. Omar lived in an apartment building on the La Brea Avenue, Coliseum Boulevard area. The entrance to his apartment was at the top of two flights of stairs.

There was a balcony overlooking a swimming pool that had been cemented over. The apartment owner had the pool covered after a child had drowned in it. Omar's door was never locked and most of the time it was filled with people. The music was always loud like there was a party. On this particular day, a group of men sat in the living room, waiting for Kojac.

Omar had a huge fish tank. He liked to raise predatory fish. The men loved to watch the feedings. Some of the men would stare at the tank as if it was a movie. Hearing the door open, Johnnie-Reb reached for his pistol. Seeing it was Kojac, he pulled his shirt back down. "It's about time you got here man."

"You're late as usual, Kojac," Omar said. "These brothers were about to leave."

"I'm here now, that's all that counts. I was with a young lady. If you had seen how fine she was, you'd understand."

"This is business, Kojac. Let's get our business taken care of before all that other bullshit." Omar said angrily. Omar had two distinct personalities. He was a kind-hearted person who would fall for any sad story. Children loved him and he always took time to play with them. Anyone could go to Omar for help and a lot of people did. He was able to help because he was a fairly big-time drug dealer and known to be a cold-blooded killer. Omar was known as the "Godfather" in the Jungle. Omar, Kojac and the other members of the gang had met in San Quentin prison. All of them were ex-cons except Johnnie-Reb.

Kojac ignored Omar and walked towards the Kitchen. "Where's Evelyn?" he asked. Evelyn was coming from the kitchen as Kojac was entering. The two met and hugged. The voices of several other females could be heard in the back. All of the women knew to stay out of the living room when Omar was conducting business. "We got business to take care of Kojac!" Omar yelled.

"You're just jealous, Omar." Evelyn said smiling and squeezing Kojac tighter.

"I'm not jealous, Marie," Omar said in a childlike tone. "Business is business."

Omar called her Marie, everyone else called her Evelyn. They had both moved to Los Angeles from Beaumont, Texas. Evelyn had always looked out for Omar, even during the years he spent in San Quentin. She liked to flirt with other men in front of Omar, as if she were trying to make him jealous. That might explain why Omar would sometimes strike her unexpectedly and without explanation. He was always sorry later and would comfort her with some kind of expensive gift. The beatings and the gifts came pretty often. She had an impressive collection of jewelry.

Kojac was from Mississippi. He was already strong and muscular before going to prison. Serving time in San Quentin had given him a body that would have qualified him for a Mr. Universe contest. He was popular with women because of his build. Women would whistle at him when they passed him on the street. Kojac considered himself a professional outlaw, bragging that he came from a long line of outlaws.

Those who knew him never trusted him alone with a woman because he was also a known rapist. There were stories about women he had raped on his short stays out of prison and stories about men the he had raped while in prison.

"I had better let you go Evelyn," Kojac said, removing his hands from Evelyn's waist. "Your old man is getting angry."

"We'll talk later," Evelyn replied, as she turned towards the kitchen.

Kojac turned to Omar. "You're too serious, man. You need to relax more."

"Forget the dumb shit, Kojac," Omar said. "Kool came up short again."

"He's not holding out on us," Johnnie-Reb interrupted. "He just keeps letting them bitches get dope from him on credit. Or for free. Either way, that's why he's always coming up short."

"How are the other guys doing?" Kojac asked.

"Everyone else is fine; we got good workers, except for Kool." Johnnie-Reb answered.

"What do you want to do, Omar? Kojac asked.

"It ain't that much money. Just don't give the fool any more dope to sell." Omar answered.

"I say we kill him!" Kojac replied nonchalantly. Johnnie-Reb could not hide his anxiety. He stood up. "Wait Kojac, it's not worth that. He's just weak for bitches, he doesn't mean nothing. I agree with Omar, let's just don't give him any more dope to sell."

Johnnie-Reb was the only native Californian in the group. He was also the only one who had not served time in San Quentin. He had been in jail a lot but he had managed to avoid prison. He did work out a lot and had muscles comparable to the ex-cons.

"His weakness is his own problem," Kojac replied. "We have to set an example if we are going to run a successful business. We should be a lot bigger than we are now. We just waste too much time playing these small-time games. The time is at hand men. We need to look into the new drugs. We need organization. We need to get our share of the money that is being passed on them streets. If we don't get it, there are some guys out there who will. As for Kool, we have put three contracts on that nigger already. Three times we said we were going to kill him. Three times we called it off. No fool should be that lucky. I want kool beat to death and I want everyone to know it was us who did it. I want the body to be left in the streets so that the word will spread around the Jungle. The pushers will think twice before crossing us and the dopeheads will know we mean business."

Omar rubbed his head. "Kool is one lucky muther-fucker. We can't keep letting him get by. I'll tell the guys to take care of him. He's history. Now, what kind of new drugs are we talking about?"

"They have been going wild over this new stuff called angle dust. The people who know how to make the stuff are making money like a muther. We need to get in on it."

"" We've been hearing about the stuff on the news. A lot of people are tripping out, going crazy and dying off that stuff. It may not be a good business to go into.

"There ain't no other way. It's the drug of choice on the streets now." Kojac's expression suddenly changed as he looked at his watch. "I got to go you guys. Let's go ahead and split the money."

Omar left the room and returned with a briefcase filled with money. He tossed stacks of bills to each of the men. Kojac put his share away and headed for the door. "Omar, tell Evelyn and the girls bye for me. I'm going to meet some people who can get us started in the angel dust business." He turned to Johnnie-Reb. "Get a couple of guys and take care of Kool." He said as he walked out of the door. He paused before he let the door close, turned and smiled. "You guys tell everybody you see. You have seen the Divine One and the time is at hand."

Kool was busy going about his morning chores when he glanced over his shoulder to notice that it was almost daybreak. Like a vampire, he had to be finished before the sun rose. As he glanced over his shoulder, he saw the security guard creeping upon him, gun drawn and pointed at his head. The guard was in the process of yelling "Freeze!"

when Kool turned on one knee and executed a Karate foot sweep. The guard was knocked from his feet, his gun flying out of his hand. Kool dropped the packages of bread and rolls he was accumulating. He quickly ran for the hole he had cut in the fence at the back of the supermarket. Once he got outside, he grabbed a box of bakery products he had placed there earlier and ran for the jungle.

Kool lived on Coliseum Street, around the corner from Omar. He was a veteran of the United States Army. He was attending school on the GI Bill; however, the educational assistance check was not enough for him to live on. Kool supported himself by pushing drugs, stealing, and doing odd jobs for the local gang leaders.

He had a fairly large number of single parents who came to him to purchase fresh bread at discounted prices. The bakery trucks delivered the baked goods to the market before dawn. The deliveryman would place the baked goods inside a fenced-off area in back of the market. Kool would wait for delivery, crawl in through a hole he had cut in the fence, and have fresh bread for sale before the market opened.

He had not stolen as much bread as he had wanted to that night however, when he got the boxes inside his apartment, he was pleased with what he had. Customers were at the door as soon as it was daylight. The women, most of them wearing robes or nightclothes, would negotiate with Kool trying to get the most bread for the least amount of money. Kool always tried to talk the women into sexual arrangements. The ones who flirted with him could talk him out of anything.

Lately he had been keeping special packages for Harriet. She lived in the same apartment building as he. He was infatuated with her and she had been getting a lot of free drugs and bread. There were other women but, Harriet was Kool's dream girl. She was light-skinned, had long hair and a dynamite body. He stood daydreaming about Harriet when the realization that the enforcers would be coming after him, made him look out of the window.

His timing was right. He was about to turn away from the window when he saw Johnnie-Reb and two other men coming through the alley across the street. Kool waited until the three men had begun to climb the stairs to his apartment before he threw down a rope and climbed from his front window to the ground below. When he touched the ground, he began running as fast as he could. He could hear the men breaking down his door as he made his escape.

Kool ran as fast and as far as he could. He was exhausted and drenched with sweat when he reached the Adams Motel. He waited and watched carefully to make sure he had not been followed, then he rented a room, found his way to the bed and passed out.

Kool slept the entire day and night. It was early the next day when he and I met in the courtyard. I was doing my morning exercised which included Martial Arts forms. He was checking the streets to see if Johnnie-Reb and the boys were on his trail. When he was satisfied that the streets were empty, he came over to speak.

"What Kind of exercise do you call that?" "This is called a form," I said. "It's Martial Arts. The Japanese word would be Kata; the Korean word is Hyung."

"I do a little Martial Art myself." Kool said as he began to execute some kicks and punches.

"What style?"

"I don't have any particular style I do a little of it all."

"I practice Tae Kwon Do," I said. "My teacher is Grand Master Sang Kyu Shim in Detroit."

"It looks like you know what you're doing. Maybe you can teach me some."

"Sure, I'm in room 208. Come up anytime."

"You get high?"

"No, I try to keep my focus on Martial Arts. I do know a couple of ladies who are looking for some weed though."

"I got just what they are looking for. If you know anybody looking for weed or cocaine, I'm your man. I'll drop by a little later."

Kool came by later that day. I introduced him to my wife Mary and our friend Mary Underwood. Kool set out a few joints to be sociable. When he found out that the ladies liked cocaine, he began to pull out his stash. As usual Mary Underwood made him pull out much more than he had intended. He was angry with himself for getting into even more financial trouble but, he was really high, the ladies were beautiful and he felt like the women were celebrities after he learned that they were both strippers.

Kool began to visit every day. He began exercising in the courtyard while I worked out. Josh, a pimp who also lived in the Motel, soon joined us. Josh shared a room with a gorgeous young lady with a fantastic body. Every morning he would send her out to walk the streets. She returned at night with money, drugs or both.

We began getting together as a group. Josh and Kool only smoked weed. The three girls liked cocaine. We all enjoyed having philosophical conversations. Josh thought that I was a pimp because there were two women with me. I was never able to convince him that Mary was my legal wife and Mary Underwood was a long-time friend. The two of them had danced together in Detroit.

Kool soon ran out of dope and money. His stay at the motel had been nice but, it was time for him to make a move. In his mind, enough time had passed for Omar and Kojac to have forgotten the matter. He decided to go back to the Jungle to find out. In reality, around three weeks had passed but, getting high interfered with Kool's ability to keep up with time. To him months had gone by.

Kool went back into the Jungle, telling his customers that he had been out of town for a few months. It took all the nerve he had to go to Omar's apartment however, he knew his life depended on him seeing Omar or Kojac before the hit men found him.

Kool took a deep breath and walked up the stairs to Omar's door. He knocked lightly on the door. "It's open!" Omar yelled from the inside. Kool hesitated. The door swung open and Kool found himself facing a gun being held by KoJac.

"You got to be one of the world's biggest fools." Kojac said as he placed the barrel on Kool's nose while he grabbed his shirt with the other hand and snatched him into the apartment. "You're supposed to be dead you know. Now I know that you're not stupid enough to come here unless you plan to pay me all of my money plus interest. Now pay up and die fool."

The room was filled with nervous men looking at Kojac and Kool in amazement. "I got robbed," Kool said nervously. "Some gang from South Central, they beat me up, took my dope and my money. I been in the hospital for over three months. I can prove it. Come on Kojac, please don't kill me man."

"Go on and shoot him before he pisses on my floor." Omar said. "We got business to take care of."

"I don't want to be involved in no murder Kojac," One of the men said. "All of us are ex-cons and you know we are not supposed to be together, let alone be around guns. We came here to sell you guys some PCP, not get involved in a fucking shooting. We can leave while you handle your business. We can come back some other time."

"Hold off a minute Kojac." Omar interrupted. "This fool may be of some use to us. What do you say we give him another chance? If he plays his cards right this time, he can pay us back and make some money for himself."

Kojac seemed to know what Omar meant. He released Kool, took a deep breath to calm himself then, walked over to a man holding a briefcase in one hand and a gun in the other. "I'm sorry for the interruption. This is not the way we usually do business. Kool is one of our employees." He turned to Kool and motioned for him to take a seat. "We are glad you guys came and we don't want to miss out on this opportunity. We've been looking for people who know how to make this PCP. The Lord works in mysterious ways though. Me, Omar, Johnnie-Reb, none of us know a damned thing about this PCP or angle dust as some call it. We have no way of knowing if your product is the real thing. Maybe the Lord sent Kool to help us out."

Kojac turned to Kool. "These gentlemen deal in PCP. It's the stuff they use to make angle dust. We're new to the business so we don't have a reliable way to test their product. I think you owe us one Kool. Test the product for us, all is forgiven. If everything is okay, we can pay these good brothers and send them on their way."

"I've heard that PCP runs people crazy," Kool said nervously. "I don't want to mess around with that stuff."

"Would you rather be crazy or dead? Your choice. Kojac said without looking at Kool."

"Okay, alright, I'll do it."

Kojac nodded to one of the men. "Show us how this works."

The man opened the briefcase and took out one of a few bottles of a clear liquid. The bottles were carefully wrapped. The man opened a bottle and inserted a dropper. He then unwrapped two small packets, one containing marijuana, the other spearmint leaves. He then filled the dropper with the liquid, placing a dropper with the liquid, placing a dropper full on the marijuana, another on the spearmint leaves. "It's called angle dust." The man said. "Some people get high with the liquid placed on the spearmint leaves, some like it on marijuana. They say the high is intensified when you put it on weed." Now, the liquid contains embalming fluid. Which one do you want to try?"

"Roll up a joint of each one." Kojac said. "Let him try them both."

Kool reluctantly took both joints. He lit one. The first puff was enough to disrupt his thinking process. His actions indicated that he was completely stoned out of his mind. He sat string at the ceiling, unable to speak or move. The men were laughing at his reactions.

Kool was unaware of anything else happening that night. Kojac had some of the men take him to his apartment where they threw him inside and he passed out on the floor. Once again, he had cheated the hit men. Omar paid the PCP dealers and made arrangements to do business with them in the future.

Angle dust sales went well in the Jungle. Kool recovered, got his job back, got himself out of debt and began to make money. Other users were not so lucky. There were a lot of deaths and injuries connected to angle dust. Along with Kool's good fortune, he also gained a fondness for angle dust. It was not long before he was smoking it with his female clients. Harriet loved it. Kool wanted to spend as much time with Harriet as he could. Harriet did not like Kool but, she liked to get high and she could not afford it. She had three children and was on welfare.

Kool was busy telling everyone that Harriet was his girl. Harriet was just as busy telling everyone that she would never have sex with Kool. Kool was bragging that they were having sex all of the time.

Harriet was a preacher's daughter. She had three children by Robert. Robert was now serving in the United States Army's Special Forces. She and her children's father planned to get married after he was discharged from the Army. His discharge had been delayed because of some trouble he had gotten into and he was now serving time in a military prison. He was soon to be released. Harriet kept an apartment for him.

Harriet and Robert had been together since high school. He had been the captain of the football team. She had been the head cheerleader. Robert was good looking and well-built. Kool was not Harriet's type. Kool had a muscular build btu he wore very thick glasses and had crooked teeth. Had he not sold drugs, she said that she would never associate with him. To keep the drugs coming, she had to make Kool believe that she liked him while she avoided sexual encounters.

Although they got high together quite often, she talked her way around Kool's sexual advances by teaching him about the Bible and telling him how her father raised her to be a good Christian. "I already have three children so; you can see I can't afford to make any mistakes." She would say. "Besides, I'm lucky enough to be engaged to their father. I'm not going to do anything to jeopardize that." Kool felt that, as long as she liked to get high, there was always a chance. Besides he loved to talk. He often told people, "I was blessed with the gift of gab. I can talk my way into anything and talk my way out of anything."

Nitro worked at the Page Four Lounge. He was a well-known bouncer. He told everyone that he was an ex-prizefighter and that is exactly what he looked like. He was big, musclebound, had facial scars and a tooth missing. He always wore a suit and tie. He regularly bought marijuana and cocaine from Kool.

Nitro considered Kool a weak man and began taking advantage by getting drugs on credit. After credit was established, he began to pay late or not at all. Kool mistakenly told Nitro that he was short on his money and could not afford to get in trouble with Omar and Kojac again. Nitro offered to help him out by sharing his apartment and sharing the rent. Instead of getting paid for his drugs, Kool ended up accepting Nitro's money as rent with a promise that drugs would be paid for at a later date. Now Nitro had the key to the apartment. He never paid for the drugs and never paid rent again.

Nitro did not show up at the apartment very often. He claimed he owned a big house in the valley and only spent time at Kool's apartment when he did not feel like driving home or, when he had met some lady at the bar and needed the place for a quickie.

Despite his problems, angle dust was selling well and Kool managed to stay in good graces with Omar and Kojac for months. Keeping Harriet high and being unable to collect rent from Nitro, things were beginning to take a turn for the worse. Just like before, it was time to pay and Kool was short. He told Harriet that he would get into trouble if he did not come up with some money. Harriet promised that she would help him pay but the money never materialized.

To make matters worse, Nitro showed up at the apartment with two women who wanted to get high. Kool was not home. Nitro tore the place apart, found Kool's drugs and helped himself. Nitro had never used angle dust. The first puff sent him into another world. He became a zombie. He could not speak or understand anything or anyone. There was nothing the girls could do to bring him around. They eventually called 911. Nitro was rushed off to the hospital. He was later placed in a mental facility where he remained in the zombie-like state for over a month.

Kool was pleased that he once again had hid apartment to himself. The problem was, there was no way to talk Kojac out of killing him this time. Kool hid out in his apartment. He did not answer the door or phone. He felt like his luck had finally run out. He constantly peeked out of the window to see if the enforcers were coming. One day he saw me passing his apartment and began to notice that I passed his place nearly every morning and returned late in the day.

Kool decided to try a disguise and follow me to my apartment one evening when I returned from my daily walk. I was limping badly as I walked up the stairs to my door. I had noticed someone following me. Thinking that it was a robbery attempt, I got ready to defend myself.

"Twenty-Five." He called from the bottom of the stairs trying to conceal himself.

"Who is that?" I answered.

"Kool. It's Kool man. Remember me? We met at the Adams Motel. You're the Karate man. You do that Tae Kwon Do stuff."

"I remember you. You're the dope man. Why are you disguising yourself?"

"People are after me. Open the door and let's get inside."

Kool followed me inside. It was just before dark. There was no electricity in my apartment. I lit a candle as he looked around in the dark for a seat.

"How long have you been here?" He asked.

"About three or four months."

"Where are those two beautiful women who were with you? You know, the dancers. Mary and Mary."

"Both gone. Mary Underwood went back to Detroit. My wife and I moved here together bur, she left."

"I live right up the street. I've been living here for years. I have the best view in the Jungle. From my apartment, I can see everything that comes in or out. I have been seeing you take long walks, leaving early in the mornings, coming home near dark."

"I'm trying to train myself to walk again and, trying to walk off depression."

"What happened? The last time I saw you, you were doing that Tae Kwon Do thing."

"I was recovering from foot surgery when we moved here. I must have done some damage though by working out too soon. My foot began to hurt at the Motel and the pain grew increasingly worse until I could not walk at all. That was shortly after you left the Motel."

"Sounds like your luck is about as bad as mine. Things were going good for me for a while. I met this fine bitch named Harriet. She's light-skinned like your wife. We really had it going on until I got into money trouble with the gang."

"Light-skinned must mean a lot to you. I have seen fine women in all colors."

"Color means everything in this country. I love high-yellow bitches but, high-yellow or not, all women are bitches. That's just the way it is."

"I guess that's why you never married. If you don't respect women, they won't respect you."

"You don't know bitches like I do. They are all yours as long as you are the man with the money. When the money's gone, the bitches are gone."

Kool's words awakened memories of my life in Detroit. I had worked in the automobile factory for the Chrysler corporation. The guys on the job would tase me about my engagement to Mary. "You know that woman is too fine for your ugly ass," my friends would say. "She won't be with you for long."

My problem was that I was afraid they were right. I was a poor country boy from Alabama. My wife-to-be was well-known as one of the finest dancers in Detroit. I had always felt that Mary was way too classy for me. I had been taught to respect my elders, though, and I always listened to the older, wiser men. Old man Reed was the wise man on the job; his advice calmed my fears. He would come to my rescue by saying, "You may not keep her long, but at least you can say you had her."

My life in Detroit had been magical. In the years I lived there, I had been transformed from a dumb country bumpkin into a well-known marital arts instructor and ladies' man. I had dated what seemed like hundreds of dancers before I asked Mary to marry me.

"Believe me," I said to Kool, "f it's one thing I know it's women. Mary and I had the perfect marriage. Then, my first wife, Minnie managed to get me tied up in the court system with a child-support case.

I ended up in jail, wondering how in the hell I got there. Everything went downhill after that. That's how we ended up out here."

"You running from the cops in Detroit?"

"Yeah," I answered. In the environment I had encountered since my arrival in Los Angeles, I did not feel it wise to say I actually came to join the Los Angeles Police Department. I had applied for the position of police officer in Detroit and Los Angeles. I had passed the written and physical test in Detroit before being told I had a child-support problem that needed to be straightened out. Finding it impossible to satisfy the Court, I decided to test in Los Angeles.

"I'm a hustler," Kool said. "I been hustling all my life. I'm always on the run. If the cops are not after me, the gangsters are. I'm going to get of this one day though. I go to school on the GI Bill. I plan to get my degree and one of them high-paying jobs. I wish I could pimp though. I know a pimp named Blue he has this blue pimped-out Cadillac. Almost everything in his apartment is blue and I just can't describe the bitches, talk about fine."

"I could never be a pimp. I love fine women, but I'm too jealous to share them with other men. I don't care how many women I have I don't want them with anyone but me."

"Well, it ain't good to be up here without lights, gas, and furniture. I can turn you on to Omar and Kojac if you want me to. They are the gang bosses in the Jungle. I can't introduce you personally right now, but I can tell you how to get in touch. You let them know you're on the run from the cops, they'll put you to work. You could sling some dope until you get on your feet."

"I don't want to sell no dope. It's bad karma. Besides, I was doing OK working. I made a good living teaching martial arts and working for Chrysler. I lived just as good as the pimps and drug dealers. I never had to do anything that would get me put into prison, and I'm too old to start now. When I get well, I'll get another job. I ain't no criminal."

"Shit, nigger, you can't survive here unless you are with some gang. We are all gang members; we don't have a choice. They already took you off the job and put you in jail. If working was the way out, there wouldn't be so many Black men in prison. The system is set up that way. For Blacks and Mexicans, it's hustle or die.'

"Not me, I worked for Chrysler for seven years. Before that, I worked for the federal government. Besides, I'm a Vietnam veteran. I believe my situation will be straightened out soon."

"How long before they evict you?"

"I don't know."

"The last time we met you didn't get high. Do you now?"

"No."

"You will before this is over," Kool said as he goat up to leave. He took out a bag of weed and two joints of angel dust. He threw them to me. "You might need these. I'll see you later. You already live like an animal, no lights or gas, soon they'll put out and you won't have a roof over your head. It may take that for you to see how system really works. Here's something for you to think about while you're doing your daily meditation. Pimp or die, nigger."

Dying was exactly what I was prepared to do, I thought as Kool left.

The events leading up to my being there were too weird to explain. The only thing that I was certain about was things were totally out of my control. I could not get rid of the fear that I had come to Los Angeles to die. I felt that my karma had forced me here, and there was no way to avoid my death.

After the pain in my foot got so bad that I could no longer work at the motel, we moved into the apartment and I applied for unemployment compensation. The State of California ruled that I should be penalized thirteen weeks of my benefits because I voluntarily quit my job with Chrysler. I was ordered to come back in thirteen weeks. At the end of the thirteen weeks, our lights and gas had been turned off. I went back to the unemployment office to be told, "We meant for you to report to the office each week during the thirteen-week penalty period." Because I had not reported back each week, my benefits were denied and all I could do was request a hearing.

I could not reapply for unemployment or apply for work because the pain in my foot had made it impossible for me to walk. I was sent to a doctor to be examined for state disability. The doctor looked at my physical build and became offended. "What's the reason you're disabled?" he asked.

"It's my foot," I answered. "I recently had surgery and the foot never healed. Standing is very painful right now."

"If you can't stand and work, you can sit and work. You are in too good a shape to be on disability. That'll be all."

Mary and I were completely out of money by that time. Mary wanted to get a job at the Page Four Lounge to keep us from starving to death. I did not agree. I did not want her back in the bars. We had agreed that she would stop when we were married.

Since my disability was due to a foot injury I received while serving in the United States Marine Corps, I wrote to President Carter about our situation. The Veterans Administration and the American Legion were contacted. The American Legion brought us some food and paid two weeks' rent. The Legion was sure I would be receiving compensation from the Veterans Administration during the two-week period. They were wrong. After the two weeks were over and the Veterans Administration had not responded, the landlord was upset, because, according to him, the American Legion would have paid a month or more if I had been a white veteran.

Mary took the job at the Page Four Lounge, but my inability to walk and her getting high and partying with her fellow employees soon got us into arguments. We thought things were changing for the better with the assistance from the American Legion. However, instead of a veteran, the Veterans Administration treated me like an enemy of the state. Finding ourselves without any means of support, Mary became paranoid. Soon, she spent her time getting high with her friends from the Page Four Lounge. Eventually, she moved in with a girlfriend.

Finding myself unable to walk and being alone in a dark cold apartment made me realize that, if I did not help myself, I would die. I had reached the point where I wanted to die. I did not want to go to hell. Life here on earth had bee too hard. There was no way I would risk going to a worse place. The thought prevented me from committing suicide. I had been taught that suicide was one sure way of going to hell.

I realized that, no matter how painful, I had to make myself walk again. I began to leave early each morning and walk as far as I could. I began reliving a time when I had been ordered to walk on an injured foot while in the Marine Corps. I went to the doctor after injuring my ankle. The doctor placed my on light duty. My commanding officer refused to honor the doctor's orders for me. In addition, he said that he was determined to teach me to function while in pain. While my foot was injured, I was ordered to carry an M-60 machine gun everywhere I went while I was on the base. This included ten-mile marches to the range. While the other Marines relieved each other every three miles, I was made to carry the gun alone the entire ten miles, both ways.

The words of my Commanding Officer turned out toe be true. "Marines have to learn to ignore pain." He would say, "I want you to carry that weapon everywhere you go. When you march to the range, your Fire Team is not to relieve each other, you carry the weapon the whole ten miles. Soon you'll learn to function without thinking about your feet hurting. One day your life may depend on it." After training, I was ordered to stand at attention for hours at a time.

I had carried around a lot of hate for my commanding officer. Now, I could not help but appreciate how I had been trained. Otherwise, I may have died alone in that empty apartment trapped by the pain in my foot. I thought about my Marine Corps training each day. I walked in pain for miles and miles every day. I would come back and practice marital arts at night until I pass out. I was on one of those walks when Kool saw me.

I had heard about angel dust. I had been afraid to try it. After Kool left the joints, I began to wonder if I would lose my mind or even die if I smoked one of the joints. Either way, it would mean an escape from the extreme depression and pain I was in. I lit the angel dust, I did not lose my thought process, but I found myself pain-free for the first time in years.

Kool began to drop by often. He would bring fresh stolen bread and for a while that was all I had to eat. He would also supply drugs, and we sat there in the dark, got high, and talked about the Bible, philosophy, and marital arts.

One day Kool came by excited about what he thought was the answer to his financial problems. He held a stack of government checks he had stolen from the mailman. "Look at this shit!" he said, unable to control his excitement. "I'm rich."

"Where did you get them?" I asked.

"The mailman was putting mail in one of the apartments on Coliseum. I passed that little mail cart and saw this big stack of welfare checks, I just looked around to see if anyone was looking. Then, swoop, I took the whole stack. You want some?"

"No thanks. I would have no way to cash them and, getting caught with one would be a federal offense. I told you, I am not a criminal. How are you going to cash them?"

"I don't know. I'm going to give Omar and Kojac a stack to clear up my debt. Then, I'll give the rest to this pimp. He'll let is bitches cash them."

Kool took the checks to Omar and Kojac. They did not accept the checks for payment but, his attempt to pay saved his life once again. They gave him a week to cash the checks and bring them the money.

Kool went to Blue for help. Blue refused the stolen checks. Another pimp agreed to take the checks for sixty percent of the value. Unable to get other offers, Kool had to accept. He gave the pimp the checks. He was told to come back in a couple of days for the money. Each day for a week, the pimp kept telling Kool to return the next day. Kool ended up getting less than five hundred dollars for the entire stack of checks. In addition, the week had passed and the contract on his life was on again. Omar had everyone in the Jungle looking for Kool. It became too dangerous for him to visit me.

GANG MEMBER

I had not eaten in a few days when I began to write President Carter again. The President had the Veterans Administration to arrange a physical examination for me. I remember the expression of the doctor when he had me to undress for the exam. I heard the man's conversation with another doctor before he came into the room. "This guy should be ashamed to talk about pain. You should see the ab muscles on him. He is as hard as a rock." Once again, a doctor was so impressed with my physique, gained from years of Martial Arts training, that there was no way he would helping me to get disability. Once again, without any examination, the doctor said that I was okay. My disability claim was denied again.

The State of California sent information about a medical card that I could get from the County Welfare Office. With the card I got a chance to see a podiatrist. The doctor examined my foot and took x-rays. He informed me that the pain was due to some type of metal wire the doctor had placed in my big toe during surgery. He felt that it was some type of clamp that had been used when too much bone had been removed from my foot.

This doctor also wrote a letter, addressed "To whom it may concern," bluntly stating that I was getting the run-around from the Veterans Administration about my disability. For me, the letter was a gift from GOD. I sent a copy to President Carter.

In order to eat, I began pushing a shopping cart and picking up cans to sell. The first time, I spent five hours picking up the cans and two hours pushing the cart to the aluminum dealer only to find out that most of the cans I had collected were not aluminum. I collected less than two dollars for my work but, I made it back to the apartment with a loaf of bread and a can of beans. Now that I knew what kind of cans to recycle, I began picking up cans every day. After the letter from the podiatrist reached President Carter's office, the President arranged for another medical examination.

Because of the treatment I had been getting from the Veterans Administration Hospital, I was apprehensive about my next visit. This time however, an angle came to my rescue. This beautiful Indian lady came into the room with a long thick braid that fell to her knees. Three male doctors, with angry expressions, followed her. The lady doctor began to examine my feet; she looked around at the men in amazement. "He does have the problems that he described!" She exclaimed.

The men looked at each other with their angry expressions turning to a look of embarrassment. They then gathered around to examine my feet. They hesitated for a moment then, all of them began to make their examinations. There was an agreement that I was disabled. The case would now be sent to a rating board to determine the compensation amount.

The employees at the Veterans Administration seemed to have been angered by my writing to President Carter and by the letter from the podiatrist stating that the Veterans Administration was giving me "the run-around." Their way of getting even was to award the least amount of compensation the government could pay. Then, the Iran hostage crisis happened and President Carter had to turn his attention to much more important affairs.

CHAPTER TWO

The Coldest Days

I found myself afraid to open my eyes when I woke up in the mornings. I was still hoping everything was a bad dream and that everything was back to normal. My fear that I had come to Los Angeles to die had become more intense.

Without lights, a radio or television, all I could do was to think. My life kept flashing before me. Nothing I had done in my life should have led me to where I was. In the world that was normal for me, I would have awakened in my penthouse apartment, Mary would have been in another room talking on the phone. On Wednesdays, I would be getting ready to teach my Martial Arts class at Grand Master Shim's Dojang. Every other day except Sundays, I was training in some other instructor's class. Grand Master Shim taught on Sundays. His classes were always filled. I never missed a class.

I had worked for Chrysler Corp for seven years beginning in 1970. Most of the time, we were on a six- or seven-day schedule. Everyone knew that I was a Martial Arts fanatic. I was teased a lot about the number of years that I had trained. "I know for a fact that you have been training for over seven years," Some would say. "If you have not learned it all by now, you can forget it."

If I missed a day's work, I would return to face the guys joking about me trying to use Martial Arts in some bar fight and loosing.

I had trained with Grand Master Shim for as long as I had worked at Chrysler. Before that, I worked for the Veterans Administration in Detroit. I transferred there from the Veterans Administration Regional Office in Montgomery, Alabama.

That transfer was due to a failed marriage. Looking back, I think that we were too young. I remember discussing the situation with my mother after the engagement. "I don't think I'm ready." I would say. My mother, the pastor of our church and all of the older people advised me to go ahead. After the marriage, I had told my wife Minnie that, I seriously did not want any children until we were able to afford a home and save enough money for the child's college education. I did not want to bring a child into this world to grow up in poverty as I had done. We had come to an agreement just before she told me that she was pregnant. "But I thought we had discussed the matter and decided that we would prepare for the child' future first." I said. "Well, I wanted a baby." She replied.

Minnie and I were both around nineteen when we got married. My son Percy was born around nine months after the marriage. In less than a year we were separated. Minnie took our son to Detroit where she had family. I transferred to Detroit to take part in my son's upbringing. Minnie got married again to a man named Rudy.

In Detroit, my girlfriend Liz and I shared an apartment. We never got married because, she was already engaged to a Marine who was serving in Viet Nam. They kept in contact and we had not planned for a baby. However, before he was discharged, my daughter Carla was born. I worked as a file clerk with Detroit's Department of Veterans Affairs. I had the look of a government worker. I kept the Marine Corps haircut. My dress was always a white shirt and tie. Liz got upset if I dressed any other way. Any spare time I had was spent practicing Martial Arts.

Chrysler Corporation paid more money than the federal government. When a job became available, I first worked for the government in the mornings and for Chrysler in the evenings. I worked both jobs for as long as I could, having two children to support. Liz began complaining that I was never home. We had met and began an affair while we both worked for the Veterans Administration in Alabama. Although she was engaged, she had moved to Detroit where she had family and we kept the affair going. Liz never meant to get pregnant or to end her engagement.

After the complaints about my working too much continued, I would explain that I had to plan for my children's futures. When I felt that the nagging was getting to me, I would send her on trips to Alabama where, I felt her family and friends would cheer her up. Eventually I began to see that the complaints would always occur when her fiancé would be home on leave in Alabama. She knew how to trick me into sending her home to spend time with him.

It was on one of those trips that my brother Ace introduced me to a stripper named Apache. Ace was dating a stripper named Mae. Mae and Apache were friends and Apache was looking for someone to date. She had been having an affair with a married man for years. She was not willing to end the affair because the man supported her son and paid her bills. Apache was the first stripper that I dated. She got her name because all of her features were Native American. She explained to me that her only interest was in having a sex partner. I felt like the luckiest man on earth.

Apache's dances always crossed the line as far as the police were concerned. She would often get arrested for her performances. She made so much money for the club that the owners would immediately get her out and she would be back dancing the same night. On some occasions, she would be arrested twice in the same night.

My whole life changed when we began dating. She danced at different clubs in Michigan and in Canada and she was very popular. She was also more beautiful than any woman that I ever dreamed I could be with. She was also fifteen years older than me and pleased with my inexperience. She began to spend a lot of time educating me about sex.

After our affair began, I started encouraging Liz to take more frequent trips to Alabama and to stay longer. The two women that

I loved, both had other lovers yet, I was very happy. Apache would always ask for money but, it never bothered me because she never asked for much and it seemed to me that she was only doing it because she knew that she could. I also had a limit to what I was willing to spend and I never exceeded it.

A lot of the guys who worked at the automobile plants frequented Apache's shows. I became popular by dating her. Everything went well until I came home from work one night to find that Liz had moved out and taken all of the furniture out of the apartment. Her fiancé had retired from the Marine Corps. Liz had arranged an apartment for him in Detroit taking all of my belongings. I was very angry at first, before I realized that I had been working two jobs and saving for a long time. I had good credit and replacing the furniture was no problem. The whole place was empty except for the refrigerator. I thought about my daughter Carla then, located Liz to have the refrigerator delivered to them. I did not want my baby to be without one and I wanted to make sure that Carla was okay.

It was after her marriage that Liz informed me that she was pregnant with my daughter Raquel. The marriage between Liz and her fiancé did not go well. The Marine did not adjust to life outside the Marine Corps. The was never a time when he was not drunk. Each night he would come home drunk, wet himself and throw up on the floor. Liz ended the relationship and applied for welfare.

Since I never complained about supporting the children, Liz thought it unfair that welfare applications were not accepted unless there was a child support case against the father. I told her that I did not mind going to the friend of the court to have payments taken out of my paychecks. I was happy that Apache and I could spend more time together. Every once in a while, she felt obligated to spend time with her wealthy married man.

There was a major change in our relationship when Earnestine began working at the same club as Apache. Earnestine was lovelier than the rest of the strippers. She was fifteen years younger than Apache. She had huge breasts and, for some reason, she was immediately attracted to me. When Earnestine an I became close friends, I was amazed at the change in Apache. Apache no longer asked me for any money and refused to allow me to even buy her cigarettes. She began to buy me gifts and there seemed to be a competition between Earnestine and Apache buying me clothes and jewelry.

My Marine Corps haircut and my dress of a white shirt and tie faded away. Where I was shy before, the strippers changed me. Before, I was afraid to talk to them, now I found myself dating them. Lots of them. I picked up the name "Twenty-Five" from the strippers. They began instructing me on how to dress and wear my hair. Soon, my hair fell below my shoulders and I became "Super Fly". As time passed, I began to look like a pimp. Adding to my image was the fact that, there were always new strippers. Each time I thought I had seen the most beautiful one, someone more beautiful would appear.

I wore stylish suits, coats, shoes and hats. I never wore the loud colors that were popular at the time though. I only wore black, brown, dark blue and grey. Beginning with Apache's sex instructions I was transformed from a country bumpkin into a player. My popularity with the strippers grew from the fact that I looked like a pimp but, always remained a gentleman. To me women were Angels. I hated pimps.

My obsessive practice in Martial Arts kept the women interested, especially now that Bruce Lee had become popular. Girls were interested in Martial Arts and Martial Artist. I could not have been happier. I had changed from being a loaner into a man with good friends at Grand Master Shim's Dojang and at Chrysler. Guys liked to hang around me because, wherever I was, there were always beautiful girls. "I just don't understand it." My friend Rob would say shaking his head. "You ain't by no means no good-looking nigger. I just can't see why these women are so crazy about you."

"Some of us have what women like, some don't. It's just that simple. I'm just blessed to be one of those they like. Besides, they know that I love them. I think all women are Angels." I would say. "You see Rob, I'm just like the Good Shepard. If just one of my ladies wanders off, I leave all of the rest until I get her back."

"Twenty-Five, you're a fool." The guys would say. "One of these days, you'll run into the wrong woman. Then you'll be sorry."

We were always laughing and joking on the job. I worked the evening shift. I went to the Dojang every morning, rushed home to shower and went to work every evening then, rushed home to shower again to get to the strip club every night. I was always bragging to the guys at work about my adventures.

Things went on like that for years. Then, just like I had sold my soul for seven years of pleasure and, the seven years were up, everything began to change. The girls who I had been dating long-term with no strings attached, began talking about wanting to get married. I had been having the time of my life meeting, dating and sleeping with some of GOD'S most beautiful creations. Then, as it had been predicted, I began to run into the wrong women.

I entered a strip club one night called the Kaweka Louge. I was dressed in all black. A stripper/waitress approached me as I took a seat at the bar. "Mister," she said. "You look like a gangster."

"Just goes to show you," I replied. "Looks can be deceiving. I'm not a gangster. I'm a preacher." She laughed.

"If you're a preacher, what are you doing in a place like this?"

"Spreading the word baby. Spreading the word." We both laughed.

Someone called for a drink and, she had to leave. I turned to the stage which was located behind the bar. I looked into the eyes of Angel for the first time. Angle was her name and she looked like an Angel. Our eyes met and we stared at each other while she danced. She then made this fantastic leap from the stage to the bar. She landed right in front of me. I was trying hard to maintain my cool image but, it was hard to hide my excitement. Angel danced the entire record right in front of me. The men were yelling in the background wile I sat there looking up between her legs. I bought her a drink after the dance. We began to date.

Other dancers began telling me to be careful with Angel. She was into things that most of them did not do. I was still a dumb ass from Alabama. I was not aware of certain things about Angel. One thing was, there was usually an older man at the bar on the nights she danced. She told me that it was her father and I never thought twice about it. I later found out that the man was her pimp.

Angel and I had got really close before I found out that she was a heroin addict. I explained to her that I had no education about hard drugs. I only knew that they were bad news. I informed her that I was uncomfortable dating anyone addicted to heroin. I did not end the relationship in time though.

Angel's pimp had become angered by our relationship. She had been sneaking out to see me against his wishes. I came home from work one night to find Angle lying in front of my apartment door. She was nearly unconscious and so badly beaten that she was almost unrecognizable, I took her to the emergency room for treatment and back to my apartment to recuperate. I was more afraid than I had ever been. If I did not do something, the pimp would have the impression that he had punked me out. For the first time since I began taking Martial Arts, I really wanted to use it. I told one of my training mates about the situation and what I had planned to do. We had trained together for years and he promised to watch my back.

We found out that the pimp frequented a strip club on Grand River Ave. He was known to have a bodyguard who watched him from a distance. My friend Humphrey was already inside when I arrived. Not many people were there and there was one man seated alone behind the pimp. We reasoned that he was watching the pimp's back. There was another big guy seated at the table with the pimp. I walked in fast and headed straight for the table. The big guy got up as I approached. He held out his hand to warn me to stay away. I grabbed his hand and executed two strong roundhouse kicks to his ribs then, one to his head. He fell to the floor unconscious.

The man in the back table got up and reached inside his coat for his gun. Humphry tapped him on the shoulder before he could pull the gun out then knocked him to the floor with a spinning heel kick. The pimp got up and reached inside his coat. I kicked the table over on him. He fell dropping his weapon. I helped him up and knocked him down again. He leaped to his feet and grabbed a chair. I kicked the chair into him and knocked him down again. I kept picking him up and knocking him down until he began to cry and beg. I walked out.

My next unpleasant experience was with Pat. Pat had the most beautiful legs I had ever seen. We were immediately attracted to each other and we got along well. We dated for a long while and I even took her home to Alabama several times and we spent time with my family. Pat had a five-year-old son and our problems started when her and her son moved in with me. For some reason, Pat had an obsession with pimps. She was delighted that I had the appearance of a pimp and some people thought that I was a pimp.

The thing that was upsetting to me was that she wanted her son to grow up to be a pimp. She dressed the five-year-old in pimp-like suits, had his ear pierced, his hair permed and, had the child wearing gold chains and watches. The child was very disobedient. On one occasion, I had come home tired and the boy wanted to play Karate. I told him that I was tired and did not feel like playing. The boy would not stop kicking me. I yelled at him and told him that if he did not stop, he would get a spanking. Pat became angry and told me that he was not my child and I had no right to discipline him. I immediately asked her to move.

My days as a player came to an end after an experience with a set of identical twins. Once again, I was at the Kaweka Lounge where I had met Angel. I met Brenda and our conversation began with me asking how a woman her size could have such huge breast. I turned to see her exact duplicate standing on the other side of me. Her twin sister Linda. Brenda and I began to date. Linda was married. I sincerely wanted to be able to brag about getting them in bed together. Linda would consider it. Brenda would not. She wanted a monogamous relationship and eventually marriage, like her sister. Keep in mind, I had been flirting with the bar maid Peaches for a long time.

I wandered into the bar one night unaware that Brenda was off. Linda informed me that Brenda was not working and that she was about to get off. She wanted to go bar hopping with me. We ended up at my apartment. I was afraid to bring up sex with her because, I felt like she would tell her sister. When things got hot, I began to wonder if I was being tricked. We ended up sleeping together and, I could now go to work and brag about sleeping with identical twins. The problem was, things did not end there.

I don't know why but sex with Linda turned out to be so much more exciting than with her twin sister. We seemed to get addicted to each other. We began seeing each other behind her twin sister's back and behind Linda's husband's back. At the club, her husband nearly walked in on us kissing in the dressing room. The twins lived in apartments right across the street from each other. After dates with Brenda, I began sneaking in back of her sister's apartment to pick her up. I did not like the sneaking around; I could not brag to the boys about it.

It was Peaches, the bar maid who informed Brenda that her twin sister was cheating on her husband with her boyfriend. Brenda went to confront her sister who was, at the time, in my apartment. My heart sank when I answered the door to find Brenda standing there. I felt lower than I had ever felt when I told Brenda that I could not let her in because I had company. I can never forget the sad look on her face knowing that, her twin sister was there.

I stopped dating anyone and kept all of my focus on Martial Arts. Before, everything had been fun. Now I had to seriously think about what I was doing. I decided to go to school, only date one woman and to spend more time with my children.

My ex-wife Minnie and I had not seen each other or made contact for over five-years. I would always pick up my son Percy from his grandmother's house. The children bragging about my apartment led Minnie to believe that I had become wealthy. I had not met Minnie's husband and was unaware that they had a child together, Antoine. I also did not know that, for some reason, she had given the child my last name.

After my son had told Minnie where I lived, I received an order to come to court. Minnie was working for the Detroit Police Department.

I went to court wondering what was going on since support for my children was deducted from my paycheck. The judge asked why I was not paying child support. I angrily presented my paystubs showing the deductions. Sure, he said, you're paying for these but you're not paying for Antoine. Who the hell is Antoine? I yelled. I never heard of any Antoine. My angry attitude mand the judge angry with me. Minnie was hoping that I could not explain the situation to the judge who, did not know that, I new nothing about Minnie and her husband's child.

Since Minnie worked for the Police, the judge disregarded my attempts at explaining that I had not seen or communicated with Minnie for over five years, that she had been married to someone else for over five years and that I sincerely knew nothing about the child. I was refused a DNA test and immediately locked up. I thought the judge was only trying to scare me when he ordered me to be locked up without the DNA test but, I was wrong.

I thought that I would be locked up for only a few hours but, I was wrong again. After the first night, I realized that I was in trouble. I knew that I was locked up illegally, I did not know what I was charged with or how long my sentence was. The next day I was sent to maximum security, possibly because the other cells were full. I spent the next few days having weird conversations with men who bragged about killing and raping. I grew so angry; I began thinking about killing the judge. Minnie was the one who had lied but, it was the judge who did not take the time to see what was happening. He believed Minnie because she worked for the police. Minnie never meant for me to go to jail. All she really wanted was to fool the judge into thinking the child was mine and trick him into making me pay support for her husband's child.

There was trouble in the house of corrections on the first day. We were given a lecture on what was expected to do and told that we were responsible for the sheets, towels and pillowcases that we found on our assigned beds. We were told that before we got out everything had to be returned. When I got to my assigned bed there was nothing there. I was looking around for the things that I was supposed to have when two men approached me and asked if I was interested in buying the items. They informed me again that I needed the sheets, pillow cases and towels before I could get out. Without them, my release would be delayed.

My anger had grown each day that I had been incarcerated. All I wanted to do was to find the gym and workout my frustrations until I could figure out how to get out.

"I was told that I would find sheets towels and pillow cases on my assigned bed." I told the men. My stuff is not here and you come to me talking about you have things to sell? I think that's my stuff. And I want it back on this bed right now." I walked close to the men as I was talking.

"Wow," one of the men said. "We got us a tough guy." I kicked him in the mouth without hesitation. The other man threw a punch but I blocked and began going from one to the other throwing kicks and punches. I was about to inflict some serious injuries when the other men began yelling for me to stop before I killed them.

I recovered the sheets and towels and no one else bothered me. Guys did come up to inquire about where I had learned Martial Arts. I tried to keep my sanity by always working out. I could not bring myself to relax. I had grown up determined to stay away from crime to avoid going to jail. I could not accept being incarcerated for nothing. I found it embarrassing to say that I was incarcerated for child support when I did not owe child support. I convinced myself that if I was going to be locked up, I would rather be locked up for killing that judge.

Every day I could hear a train go by. I decided to monitor the time and planned to escape to catch that train. On the day I had planned to go. I had one hour to wait for the train when my name was called over the speaker. I was thinking that someone had told the guards about my escape plan. I got to the office to find that someone was there to bail me out. I was so happy that I could not hold back tears. Luckily for me, it began to rain so hard that no one could notice my tears. Through the fence, the guys could see who was picking me up. It was Pat with the beautiful legs. She was driving her Cadilac. She was wearing a white jumpsuit with splits on the sides. She really looked like an Angel.

The men were going crazy. "Pimp on!" They were yelling. Some of them were so excited that they began coming up to me offering me cigarettes. Pat said that she had heard that I was locked up and she got the money to get me out. Later she wanted to get together to talk about our failed relationship. I never had any problems with Pat. I did explain that it was too hard for me to deal with a five-year old that she wanted to raise to be a pimp.

We made a date to meet at a strip club called Johnnie's Dream Bar near downtown Detroit. I thought that I had covered all of the strip clubs in Detroit but, I had never been to this one. Pat and I were having a drink when Mary walked in. For me it was love at first sight. I could not get her off my mind that entire night. All I could think about was getting back to that bar alone so that I could talk to her.

I came back a few nights later. I was surprised when Mary approached me at the pinball machine. "You broke my record," she said.

"Pardon me?" I replied. "I'm a pinball freak," she said. "I have the highest score on each of these machines. You broke my record and now I have to challenge you to a game." We became friends over the pinball machines. Later we began to date.

With Mary, life was a never-ending party. The guys at work would go crazy when Mary and some of the other dancers would bring me to work and pick me up. I talked her into joining Grand Master Shim's classes. We trained in the mornings, worked in the evenings, and partied at night. Our weekends were spent with children. Mary loved children – my children. Percy, Carla, and Raquel, and Mary's nieces and nephew, Juanita, Teresa and Nate. Before long, we had made wedding plans.

Our wedding plans had been made when, on payday, my supervisor at Chrysler informed me that the court had taken my entire paycheck. I did not know what was happening, but I confident that I would be paid the next week. Each week the supervisor would tell that the court had taken m check. It never stopped. It was to explain working all those hours and not bring home a check. My thoughts were, they know I have to have some means to survive, eventually they have to let me have some of my salary. They never stopped taking all of my check.

I went to the court to explain my situation. The court informed me that there was nothing I could do. The judge's ruling was final. Our friends began recommending lawyers. None of them would take the case. Mary and I covered the phone book without success. We did not realize at the time that lawyers avoided child support cases. There was no way I could have the case examined to show that mistakes had been made. I became very depressed.

Mary had her problems too. She had not told me that Pat had been making threatening calls. She had been telling Mary that we were still going together and that we were together when she thought I was at work. Not receiving a paycheck made the stories believable.

An old man who owned a liquor store on Woodard Avenue had offered me a chance to earn five thousand fighting in his after-hours joint. I had turned him down before but I desperately needed money at that time. I accepted the fight and won the money. The money carried me for a while, but I was still working everyday with no income.

On one occasion, Pat called me and said she needed money desperately. She had paid to get me out of jail, and I owed her. I told her that I had not been getting paid and my savings were just about gone. However, I had a few dollars if she was in trouble. I was to meet her at the bar where she danced.

When I got to the bar where she worked, two big guys were waiting for me in the parking lot. Pat had paid them to beat me up. I needed the fight to work off the anger. I knocked both the men out, then went inside to find Pat. She had left town. Before she left, she had called Mary and told her that she and I were about to have a rendezvous. She informed Mary that I would be taking money out of my account and bringing to her. Mary was aware that I had taken money from my account. I was angry, but I could not help but admire the scheme.

Shortly after that incident, I went into the hospital for foot surgery. During the time I was recuperating, the children visited every day. I smiled thinking about Mary yelling at the children. "Stop jumping on the bed, you are going to hurt his foot." The children were hurting my foot. However, they were having so much fun, I was not complaining.

These were memories of the last weekend I spent with my children. I was just getting back on my feet when we got a visit from a detective with the Detroit Police. The visit was about a five-year-old application I had filed with the Detroit Police. The detective said that black men who filed applications during the same period were denied positions because of their race. The federal government had ordered the Department to look up some of these men and ask if they were still interested in becoming policemen. I told him I was.

I passed all of the tests and got through the oral interview before being told by a captain that I had to straighten things out with the Friend of the Court. I went to the court to find out what I could do to get things straightened out. I was told that, "When a Judge makes a ruling, it can't be changed." I explained that my whole paycheck was being taken, and the case was preventing me from getting a position with the Police Department. If I could have a blood test, I could prove that I was not the father of the child named in the case. No one would believe that I had been denied a blood test. No one would believe the court had made any errors in the case.

When I got the notice to test for the Los Angeles Police, I had no choice but to try. It had become impossible for me earn a living in Detroit. I went to see Grand Master Shim before I left. I had trained with him for over seven years. I felt bad about having to leave. "Life can make many unexpected turns," Grand Master Shim said. "No matter what happens, you work out two hours every morning and two hours every night. If you do that, you'll never be a loser."

I could not leave without visiting some of the clubs I had frequented to say my goodbyes to the girls. I had made my last stop at a bar on Woodward Avenue. I was saying good-bye to Princess, a long-time friend when a fight broke out over a game of pool. A man was knocked over my table. Princess and I got up quickly, trying to avoid the drinks that were spilled. The owner pulled his shotgun and pointed it at the two big guys who were beating up on one little guy. The men told the owner to put the gun away, they were leaving.

They came over to m table, as Princess and I were helping the little guy to his feet. "We'll be waiting for you outside men," one of the men said.

"He's kind of small," I said. "Why don't you just leave him alone.?"

"This ain't your business, man," one of the men replied. "If I were you, I'd keep talking to this beautiful lady. That way, you won't get fucked up along with this punk."

"I'll walk you to your car, man," I said to the little man, ignoring the two big guys.

"Oh, we got us one of them bad mother-fuckers," one of the men replied.

'Wait!" the other man said. "I know him, that's Twenty-five, the karate man. He's the one who fucked up that pimp, Cadillac Herb."

"We're out of here," his partner replied. "We'll get you later, Rudy."

After the two men left, the little man thanked me for my help. He asked if he could buy me a drink. I told him I about to leave.

"I know you," the man said. "You're Percy's father."

"How do you know my son?" I asked.

"I've seen you before when came to pick up Percy from his grandmothers'. You've seen me there with Minnie's brother Frank, you just don't remember."

"Well, good luck, man, you take care of yourself." I turned to Princess.

"Wait!" the man said. 'My name is Rudy. You're not suppose to know this, but I have to tell you because you helped me out. Minnie and I are married. We were married nearly six years ago. I know how she got you messed up the court."

I thanked Rudy for the information, but it meant nothing to me. I was finished trying to deal with the courts in Detroit. I would try to find a lawyer in Los Angeles who would handle my wrongful incarceration case.

In Los Angeles, I passed the written test for police officer. I was told I failed the oral interview by one point. At first, I was told my status as a service-connected Disabled Veteran allowed me the points I needed to pass the interview. I was sent to get proof that I was a Disabled Veteran. When I returned with the proof, I was told the points were not allowed until the test was passed.

Mary and I began working at the motel until I began having problems from my foot surgery. From there, we had moved to the Jungle. We did not know it was called the "Jungle"; we were just looking for a Black neighborhood. The apartments there were pretty nice. I had resigned myself to the reality that I had come there to die. I knew I had not lived a good life. I was in a hurry to get it over with. I prayed that Mary would get out of there in one piece.

In the apartment, I became aware of how poor people get hooked on drugs. When Kool had provided me the drug, I knew how it felt to be both mentally relaxed and pain-free. Drugs could actually take your mind away from all your problems for a while the only thing was, when the high left, the problems returned. I realized the trip away from my problems was temporary. However, as is the case with an addict, the need to get away from reality was more important than anything else.

Without drugs, I could not get rid of the pounding headaches, uncontrollable anxiety, the mad rush of my life flashing before me, or the stabbing pain in my foot.

I followed Grand Master Shim's advice. I worked out morning and night. I tried to tire myself out enough to sleep. Each day it took more and more exercise. I kept trying harder because I dreaded being awake.

The pounding in my head must have been my blood pressure gone way up. I was lying there trying to stop the pounding when I realized there was a pounding on the door as well. I cleared my head, got up from the floor, and answered the door.

"Are you all right in there, man?" It was the apartment manager.

"I'm OK," I answered. I stumbled to the door, fumbled with the lock, and hid my eyes from the sunshine when I opened it.

"Did you hear anything from the Veterans Administration yet?"

"No, I'm still waiting."

"The building owner is getting angry about the rent. I told him that you were still waiting. The American Legion only paid two weeks rent. They really mess over Black people. If you were a White veteran, they would have paid the rent until your disability checks started."

"The way my luck has been, I don't have any reason to believe I will get any help from the Veterans Administration."

"You got letters from President Carter himself. I'm sure they won't put you out on the streets. You are a Vietnam Veteran. The Veterans Administration will come through. Watch and see."

"Thanks for the optimism. As soon as I get the rent, I'll be sure to let you know. If nothing happens, don't feel guilty about doing what you have to do."

"If I can help out in any way let me know, man. Where is your wife?"

"She's gone."

"That's a shame, man," he said, shaking his head.

The man felt sorry for me, I thought. It was amazing how reality had changed. In Detroit, the guys envied my lifestyle, here people actually felt sorry for me. I did not have time to feel sorry for myself, though. If I was going to eat that day, I thought, I had better start finding some cans.

I could take some of the pressure off my foot by leaning on the grocery cart I was pushing. The pain never stopped. I had to decide to either deal with the pain of walking or deal with hunger. The desire to deal with the hunger always won out.

As I picked up the cans to feed myself, I could not help but think of the years I had spent working. It was very hard to accept the fact that seven years with Chrysler, nearly five years with the Federal Government, and becoming disabled while serving in the Marines had all come to nothing. A few months before, I had been planning my retirement from Chrysler. Now, I was living in an apartment with no lights, gas, or furniture. I was also facing the dreaded fact that, soon, I would have to face living on the streets.

Each day seemed longer and longer, but in the end, time seemed to pass too quickly. The apartment manager made his last trip to my door. He came early that morning. "You had better get out of here," he said. "The sheriffs are on the way."

"I'm ready," I said.

"Where are you going?"

"I don't know. I am still expecting some news from the Veterans Administration, though. Could I get you to hold my mail for me? I will come by from time to time to check."

"I'd be glad to do it, man. I just wish there was something more I could do."

"You've done enough, man. Things happen like they happen. Thanks man." We shook hands, and he left.

The sheriffs were coming up the stairs as the manager was leaving. I was ready to leave. I grabbed the back pack I had in the middle of the floor and headed for the door. There were no words exchanged. I walked out of the door and down the stairs. For the first time in my life, I had no plan and nowhere to go. My future would be based on the biggest decision I had to make at that time. I stood on the street in front of the apartment, wondering whether to go to the right or to the left. I felt like I had been kicked out of the human race.

I turned to the right. Jackie Robinson Park was not too far away. I had enough gas in my car to get there, but that as far as I could make it. I lay there in my car for days, not eating and hoping I would die and get it over with.

As the days passed, I learned to use the restrooms in the park to keep myself clean. I watched the children go to and from Dorsey High School. I began to be known as "the man who lives in the park." The men who worked in the park got to know me; they would come up to the car to speak when they arrived for work. I soon found out that starving was not a good way to go.

I had never been out of work, so I knew nothing about food stamps or welfare. My first experience with unemployment benefits had turned out to be a nightmare. I decided to find a police station to inquire about getting help. There was one officer at the desk when I walked in. I explained to the officer that I was homeless and on the verge of starving to death. I asked where I could go to get some help or what could I do. The officer pulled his weapon, pointed at me, and said, "I'd advise you not to break the law." I found myself laughing.

I began picking up cans again. I lived off cans of beans and bread, sometimes a package of lunch meat. I was seated in the park eating one day when Kool showed up. He was with another man dressed in a suit.

"Hey, man," he yelled. "What are you doing over here?"

"I live here."

"I came by your place a few times before I found out that they had put you out. I've been seeing you around picking up cans."

"That's how I'm eating these days."

"This is my friend Aamez. Aamez meet Twenty-five." Aame was laughing mockingly as we shook hands. "Aamez lives in the valley. I have been slinging dope for him since Omar and Kojac started tripping on me. He deals dope like Omar and Kojac, the only thing is they operate on a bigger scale. These guys are more sophisticated than Omar and Kojac; they go to school and most of the customers are White.

"Why don't you sell dope, man, or steal or something. It looks bad, you picking up cans like that. Would you pick up cans, Kool?" Aamez asked.

"Hell no! I would rob a bank and go to jail first."

"Selling dope and stealing, is bad karma," I said.

"Well, here's another can," he said, as he walked to a can and kicked it towards me. He and Aamez were laughing uncontrollably.

"Don't do that," I said, walking towards Kool, preparing to knock his teeth out.

"Uh oh," Aamez said. "He's getting angry. We had better leave." They were about to walk away when the three of us noticed a car speeding into the parking lot. Three men jumped out, running towards us. I backed away when I saw guns in their hands. Kool and Aamez both pulled guns as they turned and ran. The men fired at them. They fired back as they ran. For a minute, the place sounded like a war zone, then Kool and Aamez seemed to vanish into thin air.

I thought about the incident when I retired into my car to sleep that night. California was like the Twilight Zone to me. The thought that I had come here to die occupied my mind again.

I spent long nights in my car trying to come up with the one event in my life that caused me to end up here. I had never done anything but work and practice martial arts. That was before I started going to the bars. It felt like I had no life until I started dating the dancers back in Detroit. As I thought about how it all began, I realized that one very important decision may have led me to what I thought was my rapidly approaching death.

Racism was a big factor. I had been discharged from the Marine Corps for Physical Disability. I had been due compensation by law. However, the White employees at the Veterans Administration in Alabama had no problem telling me, "We ain't giving no nigger no compensation."

I was working at the Regional Office when a Black man calmly approached me to ask where the Contact Office was. He smiled after I showed him the way. He held up a paper bad and told he had a surprise for them. It was later that day that I heard the man had gone into the office and pulled a gun. He said that he and his family were starving, and the Veteran Administration was denying his benefits. The story was on the news and the man got a lot of years in prison. The incident taught me to never try to deal with the government with anger. I began writing to the President presenting the facts.

I had not felt the effects of racism since I left Alabama. I made more money in Detroit than I had ever dreamed I'd make, and living good had made me forget. I had forgotten about the civil rights struggle that I grew up in. I had become completely engrossed in making money and partying. Dating the dancers was all I wanted to do.

I loved the fact that women thought I was cute; fun and sex was all that was on my mind. I was too playful and I never took anything seriously. I was having something like an affair with my supervisor Lois at the Veterans Administration in Detroit. However, I never took Lois seriously because I could not see her taking me seriously. She was too fine, too classy, and too intelligent. All during the relationship I wondered why she liked me and how long it would take her to get tired of me.

I know that I did not know the meaning of real love until I met Carri Gaites. Carri was the most beautiful woman I had met. She was really cute and, to me she was the sexiest. Her body was slim and athletic. Her hair was jet black with curls and, I could not help but stare at her every time I thought that she was not looking. She had been a track star in high school. She had a girlish laugh and beautiful pearly white teeth. She always made me feel good whenever she was close. I had too much respect for her to hit on her. I respected the fact that she had a husband; she respected the fact that Liz and I lived together. Without any spoken words, she knew that I liked her. I knew that she liked me.

Liz and I lived one block away from Carrie and her husband. We both lived in Highland Park, Michigan. Carrie and I met each morning at the bus stop. We rode the bus together to the Veterans Administration Regional Office in Detroit. We worked on the same floor.

When Carrie sat next to me on the bus, my normal thinking pattern was thrown off. It was hard for me to control my anxiety. She would place her hand on my knee and smile as we talked about television programs we had seen, movies or sports events. It took all of my strength not to stare at her while briefly stealing a glance every once in a while. With each glance, I would think that God had truly made an Angel when he made her. I felt blessed because she liked me and felt comfortable talking to me. I felt like her husband was one lucky guy.

It was very hard for me to understand the reasoning behind the signs of abuse that I began to see on Carrie. There came a time when she began trying to hide black eyes and bruises. When she began trying to have serious conversations with me about our family lives, I always changed the subject because I felt like, what went on in her husband's house was his business. There was nothing that I could do about it.

My first encounter with spousal abuse was seeing my stepfather abuse my mother. Personal experiences with abuse while I was growing up had traumatized me to the point where I never discussed the matter. I was too dumb to realize that Carrie's husband had begun suspecting that she and I were having an affair.

I could no longer keep changing the subject after she made the statement, "If I mention your name in any way, he gets angry." I was so nervous that I began sweating.

"But I don't understand," I said. "We only ride the bus to and from work together. Other than working together, we never see each other... Why would he think we were having an affair?"

"He has been insanely jealous ever since we started dating. I don't know why I married him."

"Carrie, listen to me, you have to do something. I watched my mother go through that for too long. You're just too beautiful to have your body damaged like that."

"I've been thinking about moving…. To Atlanta."

"Oh no! You're thinking about leaving?"

Carrie looked deep into my eyes. "Percy, "she said. "We need to talk. I know that you and Lois have a thing but, there are some things you should know."

"You can call me at home," I replied. "Liz went to Alabama again. She has been complaining that I work too much and never spend time with her. She says she wants to be with her family and friends for a while. I don't know when she's coming back."

"I'll call you when I can," she said as we stepped from the bus and joined the people rushing to punch the time clock. I ran fast. I did not want to get lectured again by Lois.

I worked on a floor filed with filing cabinets and women. I was the only male file clerk. In Alabama only men held the Job. Men in

Detroit could choose factory work. The factories always paid more. I was waiting for a job opening.

Lois saw me running through the file cabinets trying to get to my desk. "Percy!" she called out. The women on the floor began to look at me and tease. "Uh Oh, poor Percy is about to be spanked by his girlfriend." As usual, they were teasing and laughing as I slowly walked towards Lois's desk.

"What's the matter with you? You know better than to run in here."

"Give me a break Lois, I was just trying to get here on time."

"Yeah Percy, but Clarence talked to me again yesterday about you and…. Did you wash your face this morning? She said, taking my face in her hands and examining it like a mother would do to a child. I jerked my head away. I could feel the eyes of the girls looking at me and laughing."

"Stop embarrassing me Lois… Yes, I washed my face this morning."

"Well, I see something in your eyes… Go to the restroom wash your face and come back."

"Aw, Lois…" I replied.

"I mean it Percy. You come right back; I need to finish talking to you."

I walked slowly to the bathroom like a child. I washed my face with cold water. It calmed me. I was trying to think of something silly to say to Lois when I left the restroom. Lois was on the phone.

Frances, another file clerk, had just placed some files on Lois's desk. She was passing the restroom returning to her desk. "Damn! You look good." I said. "Just shut up Percy," she replied. "I know that you are all talk and no action."

"What do you mean?"

"You know what I mean. You always talk about what you want to do to me but when I give you the opportunity, you always have somewhere to go or something to do."

"You mean the other day when I borrowed my uncle's car?"

"That's right. When you said that you were leaving early, I got off early so that we could leave together. I was ready to hang out. You took me straight home. I wasted half a day."

"But you said that you were leaving because you were not feeling well, I thought that you were serious."

"I said that so I could get Lois to let me take off fool."

"I feel so stupid Frances. I thought you were sick for real."

"Well, you are stupid Percy."

"I'll know better next time."

Lois interrupted our conversation. "Come here Percy!" She shouted. She lowered her voice when I got to her desk but there was anger in her voice and, the girls were already giggling and joking about what was happening. "I heard what you said to Francis and I did not like it at all."

"How could you hear anything? You were talking on the phone. I was watching you the whole time."

"We will talk about this later. You really make me sick sometimes. Go back to work."

Incidents like that happened often at work. I loved the job. I even loved being teased about Lois. Carrie was always teasing me along with the other girls. This time she did not say anything. She smiled when I passed her desk but, I could tell that she was sad. On our bus ride home, she told me that she would drop by my apartment later that evening.

My brother Ace had come to visit from Alabama. He had fallen in love with Detroit and had decided to stay. He and I were drinking beer when Carrie came over. Ace was bragging about May, his new stripper girlfriend. He promised to introduce me to Apache May's friend. I was anxious to meet her because she was famous and it was coming up on my twenty fifth birthday. I had celebrating on my mind.

Carrie came to inform me that she was leaving her husband. She had decided to take the car and drive to Atlanta. She wanted me to go with her. If, for nothing else, to help her drive. Everything in me wanted to take the trip. It was the perfect opportunity to start a new life with the woman I knew I could love for the rest of my life. I told her that I could not go.

When Carrie walked out of the apartment, I knew that I would never see her again. I felt like a piece of my heart was being ripped from my chest. I told my brother that I loved her and that deep inside, I felt like we would have made the perfect couple.

"Then, why didn't you go with her?" Ace asked.

"Because I'm a coward," I said. "Things are going too well for me right now. For the first time in my life, I'm able to save money. I want to put my children through school; I don't want them to have to grow up like we did. I'm afraid to make a change."

Ace went to the refrigerator, grabbed two beers and threw me one. "Yeah man..." he said. "She's is fine... But you talk about Carrie as if you love her more than you love Liz. And I know that you are not going to leave Liz, she's your baby's mother."

I had gotten with Liz on a bet. When Liz started working for the Veterans Administration Regional Office in Alabama, she was the finest thing in the building; all of the guys were trying to get with her. She would not speak to anyone. I was too shy to join the competition so they got together and bet me one hundred dollars that I would not ask her out. I went into her office sweating like I don't know what and asked if I could take her to lunch. She laughed at me. I ran out of there as fast as I could. I felt embarrassed every time I saw her after that.

One day I had to deliver some mail to her office. I quickly put it on her desk and was about to run out when she said. "I thought you said you were taking me to lunch?"

Minnie and I were married at the time but, we had separated. Minnie's family had already moved to Detroit and she was planning to join them. Liz and I started dating. The first time we had sex we stayed in the bed for three whole days. We only got up to shower and to order food. Everyone was teasing us when we returned to work. We continued seeing each other and when I moved to Detroit, it was not hard for her to move in with me because I made it easy for her to continue seeing her fiancé when he was home on leave from the Marine Corps.

I was anxious to meet the stripper that Ace had talked about on the night I let Carrie drive to Atlanta alone. I felt guilty at first but, a couple of beers and Ace's description of the strippers made me forget quickly. I had not been in a strip club since I was in the Marine Corps. Ace and I covered a lot of them that night.

The club where May and Apache danced would be our last stop. We started out early. We had visited several clubs before midnight. Around midnight we were in Bruce's Lounge on Livernois Ave. A dancer called Gypsy came to wait on our table. To me, she was gorgeous. Her breasts were so large that I could not help but stare. Ace was drunk. He always got into arguments and fights when he was drunk. He needed someone to argue with.

"What's your name?"

"Gypsy."

"Gypsy? How the hell did you get a name like that. You ain't no damned Gypsy."

"I'm sorry if you don't like me but, what can I get you guys to drink?"

"I want a beer."

"I'll just have a coke," I replied.

"Can I see you guys' ID?"

"What the hell do you want to see our fucking IDs for?"

"Look guys, I'm not trying to give you a hard time. I have to ask for ID. My job depends on it."

"Well, I don't need o damned ID. I know who I am."

Ace was too drunk to notice the bouncers and some of the other waitresses. There was a crowd beginning to form around our table.

"I'm not pulling out any ID either," I said. "I'm twenty-five years old today and the legal age for drinking is eighteen. I know I look older than eighteen."

"If you don't want to show your IDs you'll have to go." One of the bouncers said.

Ace stood up to fight. "Wait!" The owner yelled rushing to the table." Aren't you the Karate instructor at Grand Master Shim's school?"

"Yes."

"My name is Ron," he said extending his hand. "I own the place. Gypsy didn't mean any harm. They are required to ask for ID. I'm sorry for the disturbance. Why don't you stay and have a drink on the house?"

He nodded to Gypsy. She went to get the beer and Coke.

"My name is Chris." Another waitress chimed in. "If you don't like her, I'm here for you. Did you say that this is your twenty-fifth birthday?"

"Yes, it is."

"Well, Hello Mr. Twenty-Five."

Chris had tow long braids like an Indian. Se also wore a Native American headband and outfits that game her the appearance of a Native American. Gypsy came back to the table. "I got this table, why don't you move on and tend to your own business?"

Chris gave her a nasty look, called her a bitch and left. Anyone could tell that they had a serious dislike for each other. "Here is your Coke, Twenty-Five. I hope you understand that I did not mean any harm." I felt good from the attention I was getting from Gypsy despite the disrespect she got from my brother. We stayed at Bruce's until it was time for our dates with May and Apache. Both Gypsy and Chris asked us to come back. Before we got to the exit, the two of them went into the dressing room cursing at each other and fighting. The men in the club had taken their attention away from the stage and were listening the fight.

Ace's girlfriend May was a beautiful girl. Apache on the other hand was like someone out of an adventure novel. She was nearly forty years old but she had a mystical beauty. Beautiful dark eyes, hair that fell below her waist and the perfect figure. I was enchanted from our first meeting.

Apache was a self-proclaimed nymphomaniac. After we got to know each other, she promised to teach me everything about sex. Liz was on an extended stay in Alabama. She gave me and Apache nearly four months together. Liz came back and Apache got angry because we could no longer come over whenever she wanted.

This must have been near the time her fiancé was about to be discharged from the Marine Corps. Liz had not been back too long before I came home from work to find everything in the apartment gone. My initial anger disappeared after I though about my money in the bank, good credit and a desire to redecorate. I refurnished the apartment, turning it into a playboy's pad.

Gypsy became my best friend. I began dating Chris. Gypsy informed me that her name was Dee Dee. Gypsy was her stage name. I could not help but like Dee Dee. She was always introducing me to other strippers. It began to seem as if every time Dee Dee introduced me to a dancer, me and the dancer always ended up sleeping together. I never tried to sleep with Dee Dee. I considered her my good luck charm. I eventually became somewhat afraid of her when Ace told me that she was known to practice witchcraft.

Dee Dee told me that she had indeed practiced witchcraft at one time however; she quit when she began to actually see the devil. She said that whenever she was alone, she would turn and the devil would be standing there. The sightings made her give up witchcraft. Later Dee Dee and Chris would argue about who was the first one to call me Twenty-Five.

That was how things began. Me sleeping in my car was how I ended up. The devil must have played a big part in my life as well. Only there was nothing more for me to give up. I had indeed reached my lowest point. All I had to lose now was the car in which I slept. I could survive the outdoors; I was a Marine. Privacy however, was a thing of the past. The park came alive during the day, especially after the school term ended. There were dozens of children in the City's summer programs. The young men working in the park knew that I was sleeping there.

I was lying in the car daydreaming when one of the guys tapped on the window. "I don't mean to disturb you man but, we have a children's program here. The city sends lunches for the children every day. We always have too many lunches and end up throwing the extras away. I brought one over. Me and the guys want you to know that you are welcome to one every day."

I told him thanks. At that point I could not remember when I had eaten anything but canned beans and bread. I had been lying there watching my life play backwards like a movie. It was embarrassing for me to have people feel sorry for me. I also could not tolerate people making fun of me as Kool and Aamez had done. I now had a food source and I could shower in the park's gym. I remembered Grand Master Shim's advice: "Work out two hours every morning and two hours every night. That way, you'll never be a looser."

I got out of the car and began working out. I began stretching and practicing Martial Arts all day, every day. The seven years I had spent with Grand Master Shim paid off. My skills were impressive. People began gathering around to watch. Other men who studied Martial Arts began hanging out with me. As a homeless man, I was surprised at the respect I got. I picked up a few students that I trained for free. I had matches with guys who came to challenge me. A crowd began to gather every day. We had long philosophical discussions and no one seemed to mind that I was homeless.

"It's a shame man," one of the men would say. "I'm supposed to be out looking for a job and I'm out here hanging out with you guys every day. My old lady would kill me if she found out." The summer program ended and school was back in session. Groups of kids from Dorsey began coming to watch the Martial Arts demonstrations. I began teaching some of the children. I had grown somewhat used to living in the park. I could keep clean by using the park's restroom facilities, the gym's shower and I warmed myself each day by working out.

A trumpet player came over to practice each day. I enjoyed working out to his music. I remember thinking that he was bound to be famous someday. Kool had disappeared from the scene for a long time. He was now selling drugs for Aamez while Omar and Kojac's murder contract was still in effect. Just like before, he thought that he had been gone long enough for Omar and Kojac to forget. He had to take a chance coming back into the area.

It was dark and I was trying to sleep however, I could not ignore the sounds of a struggle outside my car. Someone was being badly beaten. I covered my eyes and ears hoping the fight would move father away from my car. Then I saw Kool's face being smashed against my window. He was then thrown to the ground and three men were viciously kicking him.

"Wait!" I yelled as I got out of the car. I was nervous, afraid and, I did not want to make them angry.

"You had better go back to sleep homeless dude." One of them said.

"I'm not trying to get in your business. It's just that I know the guy and…"

"This fool is about to die," one of the men interrupted. "Don't be stupid enough to die with him. Get back in the damned car!"

The man rushed at me. I evaded his attack and pushed him to the side. He tried to punch, I blocked and pushed him away again. The other two men attacked. I tried not to hurt them at first but the attacks became more vicious. My kicks and punches began to connect. I began knocking them down each time they got up. I was surprised that they did not pull-out guns. They gave up and limped off. I helped Kool to his apartment.

CHAPTER THREE

A Real Black Mafia

"Somebody better explain to me what happened. I just cannot understand what you guys are trying to tell me. The Bible says 'Of all thy getting, get understanding' now again, why is Kool still alive when you had the fool? And why art the three of you sitting here looking like you have been bitch-slapped?" Kojac was doing the talking, Omar was shaking his head. Johnnie-Reb and two other men were sitting on the sofa with their heads down. The three of them wearing bruises.

"The guy saved him."

"Who saved him? Jesus? Was it Jesus?"

"The homeless guy who lives in the park."

"What does he look like?"

"He has long hair and he sleeps in the park. That's all we know. Oh, he knows Kung-Fu."

"Long hair? So, it is Jesus. Is that what you're trying to tell me?"

"He was too good with that Kung-Fu shit. He could have really hurt us but he didn't. That's why we didn't shoot him."

Kojac took a stance like he was preaching. "They will come claiming to be the Divine One, and they will be false prophets, the Bible says. If you guys aren't man enough to do the job, get some help. Go back to the park. If the longhaired homeless man is still there, all

I want to hear is that you beat the living shit out of him. I want him dead but I don't want him shot. Makes us look like punks. I want Kool dead. Please don't come back until the two of them are dead! You hear me? I am the only Divine one around here."

The three enforcers left the apartment. Kojac was no longer worried about Kool. I was now the man they were coming after. The three men came back with three others. It was still an easy fight for me. Grand Master Shim's teachings paid off with interest. More importantly, the men had enough respect not to shoot me.

With the report that the six men had been defeated, Kojac became concerned. He contacted a hit man he knew from San Quentin. The man owed Kojac a favor. This man looked like a killer. I was sitting in the park meditating when he approached. I could feel the atmosphere change.

"Are you the man called Twenty-Five?" He asked as he walked towards me.

"I am."

"I'm a friend of Kojac's."

"I've been looking for you."

"Kojac said that you were good at Martial Arts. He was right. I can tell that you are a real Martial Artist."

"How so?"

"Any normal person would be nervous when a stranger approaches. Especially if they knew that someone like Kojac had a beef with them. You just sat there relaxed and unmoved. I'm impressed."

"Thanks for the complement but, I know why you're here. Can we get this thing over with? I'm tired."

"I'm a real Martial Artist too. As such, I'll give you the respect of a fair fight. We'll go hand to hand." He took off his coat, folded it carefully and placed it on the ground. "If I lose, you do me a favor and go to Kojac for me. Tell him that we are even."

We gave each other time to stretch. The fight began. We both avoided a lot of strong kicks before any contact was made. He was bigger and stronger than me. I was faster. After about five minutes into the fight, I caught on to his timing. I began to catch him with every kick and punch. He bowed and gave up after I began to hold back techniques that could have killed him. He thanked me for sparing his life and left with the promise that I would not have to worry about him coming back.

A lot of guys who hung out with me during the summer were present the day Kojac himself came to the park. He ignored traffic as he walked across the street. When he got close enough for us to hear him. He began doing kung-Fu forms as he walked towards me. A loud rush of wind could be heard with each move. Everyone was impressed.

He walked straight up to me. "You must be Twenty-Five, the Divine One?"

"They do call me Twenty-Five but, Divine One might be going a little too far."

We shook hands. "My name is Kojac. I was sent here like John the Baptist. Just like John knew Jesus when he saw him. I know that you are the Divine One."

"Did you come here for a fight? I don't like playing around with religious stuff."

"Fighting you is the last thing I want to do. I saw what you did to my men and the hit man friend of mine told me about you. He gave you a lot of respect. I just want to know, what is a man with your talents doing sleeping in the park?"

"Things happen."

"Just like I thought. I bet you don't even cuss do you?"

"I have my moments."

"Where are you from Twenty-Five?"

"From Alabama originally. I did live in Detroit for the last few years."

"I'm from Mississippi myself. I knew that you were from the south. We know what being a gentleman is. We know what it means to be a real man. I would like to help. If you don't mind. They told me that you refuse to sell dope. I don't blame you for that. You should get yourself off the streets though. It's not gentleman-like. I got some ideas. If you are willing to listen."

"What kind of Ideas?"

"There is good money in fighting. I can put up say, five thousand dollars. We can let guys challenge you. You win, you get fifty dollars off the top for each fight. You lose, I lose five thousand and you probably lose your life."

I don't see any problems. I had got used to sparring everyday anyway. I guess a real fight isn't that much of a difference. I don't mind.

"Good. I'll make all the arrangements. All you have to do is win. Another thing, Kool was renting a room to some guy named Nitro. I heard that Nitro does not pay. If Nitro is gone, I'm sure Kool will rent the room to you. After all, he now owes his life to you."

"Thanks, Kojac."

"No problem Twenty-Five." Kojac turned to the men who were watching. He began talking like a preacher again. "All of you punks listen to me. Go out and tell all you see. You have seen the Divine One and, the time is at hand." He turned and walked off.

Kool got the word that Kojac had suggested he rent me the room. Trying to get on Kojac's good side, Kool came to the park to talk to me. "I've been trying to get the nigger Nitro out of my house anyway. He never paid rent. He got out of the hospital a few weeks ago after he tripped out on PCP. He owes me for dope and rent. I went to the Page Four to ask him about it and he clowned on me in front of everybody."

"You should have hit him."

"What, and get killed? You don't know Nitro. He's an ex-prizefighter and a bouncer. He gets practice beating people up every day."

"Fighting is not a talent we're born with; it's a skill that can be learned. Martial arts teach you to defend yourself against anyone."

"Don't believe what you see in the movies. I have fought a lot of martial artists. I have beaten a lot of them. I'm pretty good; I could probably beat you. I've seen your moves. My arms and legs are longer than yours. Nitro is different, he's twice my size."

GANG MEMBER

"It would take you five years to be able to fight me," I said. Kool jumped up and walked close to the other men seated in the park.

"Did you hear what this nigger said? I don't believe this shit. He said it would take me five years to kick his ass."

"Don't get me wrong," I explained. "I said you would have to train for five years to give me a good fight. You will never kick my ass."

"OK, let's go right now."

I successfully blocked and countered everything Kool managed to throw, then I kicked him around a bit to the roar of the crowd. He soon acknowledged my skill and offered to pay me to teach him how to beat Nitro. I began teaching Kool how to fight. I explained that learning to fight is different from learning real martial arts. Learning martial arts was hard and it took years. Learning to fight took less time, but it was just as hard.

Kool had already developed a dislike for me, and my becoming his teacher did not help the matter. I would let him attack, then show him a countermove. He got knocked down a lot. "It's amazing how he's able to actually execute those moves," one of the park employees remarked, as he watched one of Kool's training sessions. "I think niggers be doing a little too much execution," Kool replied sarcastically as he got up from the ground.

I was with Kool in his apartment when Nitro came by. I sat and watched as Kool asked for his key and Nitro tried to hit him. Kool kept ducking, moving, and catching Nitro with solid, painful kicks. When Nitro realized he was defeated, he reached for the key and gave it to Kool.

"Twenty-five, you'd better stop teaching this nigger that shit. You are going to get him killed." He put his finger in Kool's face. "Let me tell you something, little nigger. Them little kicks you are doing ain't hurting me, you know I'll just give you the key and leave because I don't want to have to really hurt you."

Kool's whole spirit changed after he defeated Nitro. He had accomplished something he never thought he would be able to do. "It was a decent fight, "I said.

"You had better be careful. I'm getting better and better every day. You may be next on the list. Here is your key," he said, throwing the key to me.

I was very thankful. I was living inside once again; I could lock myself inside away from the world and I could once again write to the President for help.

My early morning workouts in the park became a habit. I would leave the apartment every day, headed for the park. There I earned my living by fighting. Guys began coming from all over to try their skills. Eventually I lost count of the fights.

Kojac introduced me to Omar. Omar and Evelyn were very likeable people. Evelyn loved to cook. Kojac's wife Debra visited often. They began inviting me over for dinner on a regular basis. There were always pretty women at Omar's place. Omar was like a real godfather. It was amazing to see people coming to him with their problems. Sometimes I felt like I had somehow landed in the middle of a gangster movie, only everything was real. Omar had sharks in a fish tank. The guys would get excited about feeding time. The women did not like it.

Sometimes a stranger would show up and you would hear a conversation like, "Omar, you and me were Quentin together, man. We know how it is out there, man. I need some help, brother. Do you know what I mean, I need some help?"

"Calm down," Omar would say. "I know a guy who has a little warehouse robbery set up. I'll talk to him and tell him to let you in on it, as a favor to me."

"Thanks, Omar. I owe you man."

When I got to know them, I found out that Omar and Kojac had other homes and women that they were supporting. They would sometimes stop by with money, food, drugs, or gifts of flowers and jewelry. Evelyn and I became friends.

Evelyn had a large collection of jewelry. She told me about the gifts Omar brought after he had bee abusive. I suggested to Evelyn that she start taking martial arts lessons. That way she could defend herself from Omar's attacks. She agreed. I began coming by to give Evelyn her lessons three times a week. I began meeting other women who were interested in classes.

Things worked out OK with Kool. I only slept in the apartment. I got up early and headed for the park early each day. Aamez came by after I had moved in. He began to look through my things. He opened a jewelry box that Mary had given me as a gift.

"Don't touch that," I said.

"Don't worry, man, I'm just looking. Wow, you have some nice stuff. You know it looks like you were telling the truth when you said you were a player in Detroit."

"I'm going to ask you one more time to leave my things alone."

"Why are you always getting mad? I'm just looking," Aamez said, as he continued to go through my jewelry box. I got up and walked towards Aamez. He placed his hand inside his coat.

"I don't like sissies like you," I said, walking up to him. He backed up to the wall. "You always look for trouble, trying to prove you're tough. Then when trouble comes, all you know to do is to pull your guns." I slapped Aamez hard. He pulled the gun from his coat. I took it out of hand and slapped him again. He slid down the wall and covered his face.

"Now you are lost. As bad as you are, you are about to piss on yourself because now you are about to be killed with your own gun."

"Don't kill him, Twenty-five!!!" Kool yelled. "He didn't mean anything. He was just playing."

I put his gun to his head. He was shaking uncontrollably. "Since I pay half the rent here, I expect some privacy. You can come to see Kool and go through his stuff anytime you want. Stay away from me, and my things. Do you understand?"

"Yes, yes, I understand."

I turned the gun around and handed it to Aamez. "Go find someone to play with." He scrambled out the door. Kool followed behind.

Before the door could close, Kool grabbed Aamez by the back of his coat and jerked him back inside. He frantically told us to be quiet.

We heard the footsteps of someone coming up the stairs. Kool ducked down and put his ear to the door. There were several knocks, then the person left.

"I thought you had worked things out with Kojac," I said. "I have," Kool replied, "that's somebody else." Kool and Aamez waited for the person to leave, then they left.

I looked at the jewelry box that Mary had bought for me. I sat on the floor, thinking about the life I had been robbed of. I thought about my children and our nieces and nephews. I was thinking how weird my life had become. My thoughts were interrupted when I heard the same footsteps coming to the door again. I got up to answer.

There was well-dressed Black man at the door. He spoke with a Jamaican accent. "Good morning," he said. "I am the building owner. I am looking for Dwayne." "You mean Kool," I said. "Yes. Is he here?"

"No. He left a little while ago."

"Can you give him a message for me?"

"Sure, what's the message?"

"Tell him that the rent is now too far past due; I'll have to take some action."

"Wait a minute. I share this apartment with Kool, or Dwayne, whatever his name is. I pay half the rent. I don't want to get kicked out unexpectedly."

"I haven't gotten any rent for over six months. I haven't been able to get in touch with Dwayne for three months. I'm going to start eviction procedures."

"Look," I said. "I know you won't understand this, but I was homeless before I rented this place. It is not good being homeless. I'm a disabled veteran and I don't have any definite income right now, but I can pay you some rent and some of the back rent to keep the place."

"I don't mind renting the place to someone who will pay. I am not going to continue renting to Dwayne. I'll have the sheriff come up to change the locks. You can take the place after he's officially out. The apartment is yours as long as you pay the rent and keep him away from the place. I want it understood," he said emphatically. "Dwayne cannot live here."

Events took place just like the man said. The sheriffs came; Kool was evicted; the locks were changed, and I had my own place once again.

Kool, on the other hand, could not get any drugs to sell. Blue had become more involved with decision-making. He advised Omar and Kojac not to give Kool any more drugs to sell. The organization was growing, and Kool could not be trusted.

It did not take Kool long to get into trouble with Aamez. This time, he was more down on his luck then he had ever been. He approached me about letting him sneak into the apartment to sleep and shower. I told him that breaking my agreement with the owner would mean, I would get kicked out. I was not willing to take the chance. Before long, Kool was sleeping in the park.

CHAPTER FOUR

The Hit

"That's a cop." Blue said. "You guys are just stupid. I'm not going anywhere near him. I'll be laughing when all of you go back to Quintin."

"Twenty-Five ain't no cop," Omar chimed in. "He gets high too much. Cops can't do that. If you were a cop, would you take a chance smoking angle dust? Hell, he slept in the park for months. Would a cop live in the park?"

"I've seen how good he is in Karate. The only way you can get that good is to be trained by the government. Look at his car. Homeless people live in old cars. His car is practically new. And let's look at the obvious. If I had those skills, I would just kick somebody in the head and take their money. Wouldn't you? Mark my word. Twenty-Five is a cop."

The room was silent for a while. Kojac spoke out. "Twenty-Five ain't no cop."

"Well, just do me one favor, let's investigate before we let him know too much of our business. That's all I'm saying."

"It wouldn't hurt," Omar said. "It's always better to play it safe. He is a rather strange guy."

Kojac went into his preaching mode. "He's the Divine One. I keep telling you guys. You are just non-believers."

"He's the Divine Cop." Blue said. "The reason he can smoke angle dust and still function is, he doesn't really smoke it. Don't you see. Mark my words, I know a cop when I see one. Think about this; how many homeless people get letters from the Office of the President?"

I spent more time in the apartment, now that I had my own place. Sometimes I even dressed like I did back in Detroit. No matter how things changed for the better, I always ended up thinking about Mary. Omar sensed my sadness.

"I know what you're thinking little brother," He would say. "Go on; use one of the phones in the bedroom. See if you can get in touch with your wife."

Since Kool was the only one who had really met Mary, the only thing they knew about her was what I had told them. When I mentioned that she had worked at the Page Four Lounge, Kojac questioned Nitro about her.

"Yeah, I know Mary. She's light skinned and talks really cool. She's from Detroit." Nitro said that she had quit some time ago. He promised to keep asking around.

There were so many fine women claiming to be Omar's sisters and cousins that I never knew if they were telling the truth. I was in the apartment ne night when Omar got a distress call from Wesley. She was leaving her husband. She had rented a cheap motel room in downtown Los Angeles. She was afraid and wanted to come to his place for a few days. Omar asked me to go pick her up.

I was parked in front of the motel waiting when the police pulled up behind me. "What are you doing here? Don't you know that this is a no-parking zone?"

"I'm just waiting for a lady."

"Oh, you're pimping ladies down here?"

"I'm not a pimp, I'm doing a friend a favor."

I gave a sigh of relief when Wesley came out with her luggage. The police watched as I helped her into the car.

I felt like an idiot when we got inside the car. Wesley was an aerobic instructor. She was over six feet tall and had the body of an aerobic instructor. I found it hard to hold a conversation at first but, she was friendly. I was totally at ease by the time we got back to Omar's.

I began going to Omar's to see Wesley. She began coming to my apartment to see me. We both talked about our spouses and the decisions that we had to make about them. Eventually we started an affair.

I was still faced with challenges in the park. Things were changing though. The crowds were growing larger and the police had began patrolling when the crowds gathered. With the police breaking up the crowds, there were fewer matches.

One day I was approached by the director of the park. He introduced himself and told me that he had witnessed a lot of good fights and had seen me workout. He felt that Martial Arts would be a good thing to teach the children. He asked if I was interested in teaching classes in a building in the park. I accepted his offer.

When we talked about pay, he asked if I wanted to apply to work for the city. I told him that the government had been taking my paychecks in Detroit and I could not be sure that they would not do it if they found out that I was working in Los Angeles. Working for the city might not be a good idea. The Director allowed me to teach in the building and to collect fees as my salary. He arranged for the classes to be advertised in the community newspaper.

Kool was now experiencing what it was like living in the park. Knowing that I occupied what used to be his apartment made his hatred for me grow. He came one day to challenge me to a match. I easily beat him. He promised that he would go away to train then, come back for a rematch.

Kool knew my schedule. He decided to break into the apartment while I was in the park. I noticed that the place had been broken into but, I could not find anything missing. Kool had gone through my papers and found a card from the Los Angeles Police Department. The card read: "Congratulations, you have passed the written portion of the Police Examination." Kool immediately took the card to Blue. For

Blue, this was the proof he needed to show that he was right about me being a cop.

The morning after my apartment had been broken into, I got into my car to find that someone had broken into it as well. They had tried to remove the tape player but had not finished. There were screws laying on the floor where the thief had been working.

I mentioned the break-ins to Kojac. "Why don't you come over to Omar's around noon tomorrow. We'll find out what's going on."

When I got to Omar's place, there were a lot of people and a lot of sadness in the air. "What's the matter with everyone?" I asked. The men began shaking their heads. No one spoke for a while then, Omar said. "Kojac raped Debra."

"Wait," I said. "Isn't Debra his wife?"

"Yeah… Marie, Wesley and some of the other girls went to the apartment to see her. He left her tied up and bleeding from the anus."

"Kojac is crazy," one of the men said. "He's too used to San Quentin. His mind ain't right for the outside."

All of the men in the apartment worked for Omar and Kojac. Everything got quiet when we heard people coming up the steps. There were five young men coming into the apartment followed by Kojac. Everyone greeted Kojac as if nothing had happened.

Kojac was the first to speak. "You guys have a seat." You could see the fear in the eyes of the men who accompanied him. Kojac stood in front of them and pointed his finger at them. "Last night someone broke into Twenty-Five's car. We know who the men are who are stealing these tape players. Now, let it be known that if my car, Twenty-Five's car Omar's car or a car owned by anyone in this room is touched, we are going to kill all of you. You guys catch my drift?"

The men all agreed and hurried out of the apartment. Then he addressed the men who remained in the room. "This is Twenty-Five. He is one of us now. From now on, in this organization, his word is law. The chain of command is this: Omar, me then, Twenty-Five. Twenty-Five is third in command. Everyone got that."

"Twenty-Five, that's a name?" one of them asked. "What's your last name then?"

"Five fool!!" someone answered. Everyone laughed. Kojac spoke again.

"Twenty-Five, we have an organization here. A tightly knit organization. We are going to take over the drug, prostitution, a little of everything. We welcome you into our organization."

"No offense," I said. "But I don't do crime. It's bad Karma." Everyone laughed again.

"You don't have to do anything that you don't want to do. Mainly, we just look out for each other. That's all we really expect, that we got each other's backs when the going gets rough. The way you fight, you don't have to rob or sell drugs; if you just watch my back, I'll be happy."

A young man came running to the door. He rushed in and whispered something to Kojac. Kojac whispered something back. The man ran back out of the door.

"There's a white man in the Jungle flashing a ton of money. Two of you guys go and take care of that."

Two of the men got up and ran out of the apartment. Kojac resumed his conversation. "We are about to go into something that is going to make all of us rich. The new thing on the street is called Sherm. It's a Sherman cigarette dipped in PCP. They sell like mad. We are trying hard to find out how to make the stuff but, in the meantime, we got some pretty reliable people to buy it from."

"They say, Sherm is worse than angle dust. A lot of people die from using it." One of the men commented.

"They will die no matter who sells it to them. The Bible says, 'those who will die, shall die. In the meantime, let the dead bury the dead. Let us make some money."

Omar changed the subject. "I got something I want cleared up. Twenty-Five, you have been teaching these women Karate. I don't think that's right."

"That's right, Twenty-Five." Kojac agreed. "These women don't need to know that stuff. Pretty soon they'll be using it on us."

"Martial Arts is what I do, if someone asks me to teach them, I will. You guys have to get that straight with your women."

"Let me put it this way," Omar answered. "You can teach it if you want, if my woman uses it on me, I'm coming to get you."

"All I can tell you is this. If you come, don't miss because I won't." We stood there looking into each other's eyes. Omar walked away shaking his head. "This dude is crazy man."

"That's why I made him one of us," Kojac said. "You guys see what I'm talking about? No fear, the Divine One has no fear."

The men who left earlier came back breathless and happy. They handed Kojac some stacks of money. Kojac quickly counted the money and separated it into equal stacks. He threw each of us a stack of bills. I jumped when he threw one to me.

"I don't want that," I said. "Did you guys just rob somebody? Did you kill him."

"Nobody killed anybody." Kojac said laughing. They all began cracking up.

"And you guys call me crazy? I feel like I'm in one of those western movies where, a man comes from the civilized east to the wild west. You guys are crazy." I got up and walked out of the door. Blue and three of his women were coming to see Omar and Kojac. When he saw me, he and the women turned and went the other way. He avoided eye contact. I smelled trouble.

I went to my apartment and worked out well into the night. For some reason, it was hard for me to relax. I could sense that something was about to happen. It was late when I heard a knock at the door.

"Who's there?"

"Harriet."

I opened the door. "Hello Harriet." She gave me the smile of approval that women give men when they like the way they look. I smiled back. "Can I help you?

"Where's Kool?"

"Oh, you're Kool's girlfriend. I'm sorry. Kool no longer lives here."

"Girlfriend?" She asked laughing.

"Yes, he said he had a girlfriend named Harriet who lives in this building."

"Well, I can assure you I'm not Kool's girlfriend."

"I'm sorry. My name is Twenty-Five."

"Oh, you're the Karate man."

"I guess."

"I was looking for Kool so that I can get some Sherm. Do you know where I can get some?"

"Omar probably has some. I don't sell it."

"Do you get high?"

"Yes."

"When I find some, I'll come up and we can get high together. Kool told me a lot about you."

"I'll be looking forward to it."

After Harriet left, I tried to meditate. I could not shake off the feeling of uneasiness. I got the distinct feeling that maybe this was my night to die. Then came the knock at the door.

"Come in." I yelled. Kojac opened the door and slowly walked in. "What's going on Twenty-Five?"

"What's happening with you?"

"Nothing. Look, why don't you come with me. Let's go to get something to eat."

"I'm not hungry."

"Come on, let's walk over to Omar's. We want to take you to dinner." That was the first time I had seen Kojac nervous.

"You seem nervous Kojac. It's not like you. I know what you came here for. Matter of fact I probably should have killed you when you came to the door but, it's your lucky night. If you got to shoot. Shoot. I just don't want to go to jail and, I'm tired of fighting."

Kojac took a deep breath that seemed to calm his nervousness. "It's just like they say, you're the bravest little nigger I ever seen too. And, you ain't no cop are you."

"Hell no! I ain't no cop."

"That's what this thing is all about Twenty-Five. Blue thinks you're a cop. Kool broke into your apartment and found some card from LAPD. The card said that you passed the test to be a cop. He's been spreading that lie around the Jungle."

"I passed test for a lot of jobs when I moved here. I did fail the oral test though. All they really want to know is if you'll report them if you see them committing a crime. Just like another gang. If I had any kind of job, I sure wouldn't be living here in the Jungle, hanging out with you criminals"

Kojac laughed. "I told that fool Blue, that you were no cop. I had better straighten this thing out with Blue and the boys. They should have known that anything from Kool needs to be checked out. You get a good night's sleep Twenty-Five; I'm going to find me a woman."

I thought a lot about my feeling of impending death. My spiritual beliefs seriously increased that night. After that night, I found myself with two new friends. Harriet and Blue. Blue was a pimp who surrounded himself with gorgeous women. His apartment was in the same building as Omar's. There was always a gay muscle-bound bodyguard walking behind him. There were always at least two beautiful girls on each arm. Blue apologized to me for thinking that I was a cop. He planned a party in my honor as a peace offering. Kool was ordered to stay out of the Jungle.

Kool became obsessed with taking revenge on me, Kojac and Omar. After a few weeks of training, he showed up outside my apartment to challenge me to another fight. I beat him easily again. He ventured off into Compton to find some fighters who were tough enough to beat Kojac and me and brave enough to bring a gang fight to the Jungle. He had to have a hell of a story but, as he said, he had the gift of gab. The men showed up at Blue's party intending to turn it out.

Our gang's security warned us the minute the men entered the Jungle. Kojac and I stood side by side in the middle of the swimming pool that had been cemented over. As soon as the men entered the apartment complex they charged. The balcony was filled with people from the party. There were at least ten men that Kojac and I fought that night. Omar's next door neighbor Glenda, was yelling with the excitement of someone watching a professional sports event.

The fight went on for nearly ten minutes. Four of the men from Compton lay on the ground unconscious when Someone yelled: "Police!" Everyone disappeared except for me, Kojac and the four unconscious men laying on the ground. A gang of policemen walked into the pool area with their guns drawn. Kojac and I stood side by side in the same spot where we had met the gang from Compton. The men lying on the ground began to stir.

"We heard there was a fight going on in here." One of the officers said.

"There was."

"We heard there were guns."

"This was man to man," Kojac answered. "No guns."

"What about them?" The officer asked pointing at the men lying on the ground.

"A little too much to drink." Kojac answered. "They'll be alright."

"Well, if there are no guns, you gentlemen have a good night." They looked like a movie moving backwards with the guns still drawn.

"What just happened?" I asked. "If we had been in Detroit, we would have been in jail."

"There is a 'Mutual Combat' law here. You can fight man to man as much as you want. The cops won't get involved unless someone pulls a gun."

We turned to see Glinda looking down at us from the balcony. "I've never seen anything like that. I like what I saw here tonight. I really like it. Twenty-Five why don't you come up for a drink sometime? People were coming out of Blue's apartment shaking our hands and patting us on the back.

Harriet was at the party. She put her arms around my neck in a sexy way, told me that she had some Sherm and asked me to go back to our apartment building to get high. We left.

Sherm was the name given to the Sherman cigarette dipped in PCP. The mixture of the tobacco and the PCP produced a different high than angle dust. Sometimes the side effects were amazing. The drug was sometimes known to completely change one's personality and sometimes even physical appearances. Harriet and I had stayed up late into the night talking and smoking. Suddenly and, without warning, everything about her changed. She left the room, returned in a different outfit, grabbed my hand and asked me to go with her.

We ended up at Thrifty's drug store on La Brea Avenue. I asked her what she wanted to buy but she was in a daze. She began stuffing stuff into her coat. She went from aisle to aisle stealing stuff. There was no way that people could not see her. "Wait Harriet." I said nervously. "I'm not into shoplifting." She laughed uncontrollably. "Let's go." She said grabbing me by the hand. We quickly walked out of the store. I was amazed that we were not stopped.

"Did you get anything?" She asked when we got outside.

"No! I told you that I do not do shoplifting." She began laughing again.

"I like you. Let's go back to your place and have sex."

Harriet frequently came by my apartment after that night. I learned about her children's father. She said that he had gotten involved in some kind of drug deal in the Army. He was just about to be discharged when he was arrested. He was now serving time in a military prison. His sentence would be up soon. His dealings would have resulted in years in prison however, there were some high-ranking officers involved. Some of the crimes were covered up to protect them.

Kojac continued looking for the recipe for PCP. In the meantime, he continued to use the same suppliers. As sales increased their prices got higher. Kojac became angry. He asked me to ride along with him to have a business meeting with the suppliers. We drove to a place near Crenshaw Boulevard and Florence Avenue. The men inside looked tougher than the men who hung out at Omar's.

"So… What's the reason for the price increase this time?"

"Cost of living nigger. You guys are doing alright. We hear things."

"So, you're raising the price because you hear that we are making money?"

"I'm raising the price because I want to raise the price. Do you want the shit or not?"

"We'll take it this time. I'm just letting you know that as soon as we find another supplier, we're through doing business."

"You won't find a better deal and, soon you won't be able to find another supplier. We're expanding. We plan to be the major suppliers for this whole area. You deal with us or, you don't deal."

"Me and Twenty-Five don't want to hear about your dreams and ambitions. Give me the shit so that we can get out of here."

"I wouldn't talk so tough if I were you. You forgot to bring backup. Or are you guys strapped? You set out the money, then you get the shit."

Kojac reached into his pocket and pulled out a stack of bills. There were four men in the room. Each man pulled a gun as Kojac's hand moved.

"We never bring back-up or pistols when we're dealing with bitches. You can put your manhood away. We came here to do business, not to fight."

Kojac threw the money on the coffee table in front of the man doing most of the talking. All of the men replaced their weapons. One of the men got up and went into the next room. He returned with a brown grocery bag neatly folded over from the top. The bag contained a glass quart-sized jar filled with PCP.

As the man handed the bag to Kojac. Kojac hit him hard knocking him against the wall. The man never got up. He kicked the coffee table over on the man sitting behind it, interrupting his reach for his weapon. I made a flying leap onto the two men seated on the couch as they reached for their weapons. The three of us turned the couch over. I quickly hit the one closest to me then picked up a heavy glass ashtray and struck the other man in the forehead. Two of the men got up and ran from the apartment. Kojac had picked up the other man's gun and was holding it to his head.

"Hey, hey, take it easy Kojac. What are we doing here man? We're friends. We both did time in Quentin together. What's this all about?"

Kojac never said a word. His hand began to squeezed the trigger. I was terrified. "I'll tell you what," the man said trembling and sweating profusely. "Why don't you take this batch on the house?" He slowly reached for the money on the floor and handed it to Kojac.

Kojac moved his finger away from the trigger and placed the gun in his belt. "Nice doing business with you. bitch!" I let out a loud sigh of relief when Kojac started for the door. "Let's get out of here, Twenty-five."

"Kojac, the next time you have something like that planned, please let me know. It was just luck that let me get to those two guys before the got the guns out."

"Wasn't no luck. They can't kill us. These punks coming along today have to have guns. Without guns they ain't men but even with guns, they are bitches when they come up against us Twenty-Five. If I thought they were capable of giving us any trouble, I would have prepared. When I say that we are Divine. I mean it."

On our way back to the Jungle, Kojac talked about how he planned to take over the drugs, prostitution, and robbery operations. "We will have the workers selling dope on the streets and Blue and his women can sell some too. They can do business in the nightclubs. Our organization will have to get stronger if we are going to have to deal with punks like the ones we just left. The next thing you know, they'll want us to work for them. We'll get some ledgers. We'll keep our employee's names in one. Our business associates in another."

"I wouldn't keep ledgers Kojac. Ledgers are only evidence. You know everybody and, you know when someone is late with the payments. You don't need books. Keep the numbers in your head."

"You're right Twenty-Five. We would be collecting evidence on ourselves."

We both got nervous when a police car pulled up behind us. We had just entered the Jungle. We were driving at a slow rate of speed and the car had followed us for blocks.

"We got a lot of shit in this car and this stuff carries a lot of time. We might have to fight our way out of this Twenty-Five I know you don't want to shoot it out with the cops but, It's either that or San Quentin."

Kojac pulled the gun from his belt and produced another from beneath the seat. One he pushed towards me, the other he placed under his thigh. "Turn right at the next corner," I said. "Let's see if they still follow us."

"No. I'm going to turn left."

"You're already in the right lane man. Make the right turn."

Just about that time, the lights and sirens came on. Kojac and I looked at each other as he pulled the car to the curb. The police car sped up, passed us and kept going.

"Man, that was scary. We got enough stuff in this car to get us fifty years in San Quentin at the very least."

"You would be right at home."

"You would fit right in yourself Twenty-Five You don't know it but, you're just like us."

Wesley eventually went back to her husband. Harriet kept visiting. I found it amusing that she liked to talk about the Bible when she was high. I remember laughing when she told me how we would be allowed to smoke a little Sherm in Heaven.

Harriet bragged a lot about her children's father and the good times they had before he joined the Army. I bragged about Mary and the good times we had in Detroit.

My classes in the park were going well. Johnnie-Reb became my star pupil and assistant instructor. We became well known and a lot of stories spread about Martial Artist coming to the school to test their skills against us. Some of the stories were true, others were made up. Their made-up stories were more exciting because there was a lot of exaggeration.

Johnnie-Reb warned me about police beatings. He began studying Martial Arts after he had been picked up and beaten by cops wearing KKK arm bands. I had witnessed one of the beatings shortly after I moved to Los Angeles. During our stay at the Adams Motel; I walked outside one night to investigate some noises I heard in the alley.

I saw several white policemen beating a skinny black man. They were laughing and having fun. After the man was unconscious, a female cop placed her foot on the man's head as if she were posing for a picture. When I got close to the scene, the policemen pointed guns at me and told me to get the fuck out of there.

The more time I spent at the school, the less I saw Omar and Kojac. Each time I visited, there was another story about Kojac. Omar had enlisted the help of three Hispanic men to help him do a robbery. They were waiting for Kojac to join them. One of the men was telling how Kojac had forced him to assist in the robbery of a drug dealer. Kojac found the dealer in bed with a woman. After taking the money and drugs, his accomplice was begging him to leave. Kojac decided to stay and rape the woman while the man watched, then he raped the man.

"Kojac stayed in prison too long," I said. "His mind is warped."

"I don't think that's it," Omar replied. "Kojac was raping before he went to prison."

"Kojac raped him." One of the Hispanic men replied, pointing at one of his companions. Omar and I looked at each other and shook our heads.

"Well, I've heard enough," I said. "I'm going back to the park to work out."

"Come over on the weekend Twenty-Five," Omar yelled as I walked down the steps. "The girls are having a lingerie party."

I did return that Friday night and the lingerie party was hot. When I walked in, a well-built lady was modeling a sheer silk outfit. I couldn't take my eyes off her. Evelyn was telling Omar and me that the party was for women only, we had to leave. The women were giggling. They did not seem to mine our presence.

Omar and were begging the women to let us stay when a young man came running to tell us that one of my students had broken his arm. We called the ambulance and followed the man through the alley where we met the injured child being helped by some other boys. I ran to the boy, piked him up and carried him through the alley towards Omar's place. A crowd followed.

Through the crowd, I heard Harriet calling my name. I looked to see her coming towards her. She was accompanied by three men in military clothes. I suspected one of them was her children's father. He was tall good-looking and well built.

"I've got to get to Omar's," I said. Walking as fast as I could with the child in my arms." An ambulance is on the way."

Suddenly, the man slapped Harriet so hard that both her feet left the ground. She fell hard. The man then picked her up by one arm and slapped her down again. "Get up!" He yelled. I could tell she was too embarrassed to cry. The three men looked at me and smiled as if the beating had taken place for my benefit. I hesitated for a moment, me and the men looked into each other's eyes. I looked at the child in my arms and hurried away.

I was back at Omar's the next day trying to find out who the woman was who was modeling the black nightgown. Evelyn was teasing me about the woman because she had asked for my number. "Twenty-Five, whatever you have that turns these women on like that, you should bottle it and, sell it. Boy, you would be rich. These women are crazy about you."

"I don't understand it, Evelyn. Why do women love gangsters?"

"It's different with you. You never let yourself get corrupt."

"Don't want to go to hell," I said.

Evelyn also informed me that Harriet's fiancé was in town. He was the man who had slapped her in the alley.

The more time I spent with my students, the less time I wanted to spend with my fellow gang members. I respected them as friends and brothers, however, I could not escape the fact that I thought they were a bad influence on my students. My visits grew less frequent. I also did not care for them hanging around my classes. The whole situation was confusing for me. I had developed a great deal of respect for my fellow gang members, more respect than I had for those who considered themselves model citizens. At the same time, I did not want them around my students.

On my way to the laundry one day, I discovered the value of being connected. I walked out of my apartment with a pillow case filled with dirty clothes. I was waiting to cross the street when a police car pulled up in front of me. "What's in the bag?" One of the officers asked.

"Dirty cloths."

"What's your name?"

"Percy Brown."

"Do you have any ID?" I pulled out my wallet and presented my driver's license.

"Get in the car."

When I got into the car, the two officers began laughing. "You're going for the ride of your life." One of them said. It was then I noticed the Klu Klux Klan arm bands on their arms.

They pulled off but had not gone a block before Kojac pulled up in front of their car and blocked it. Kojac did not get out but Johnnie-Reb drove up in another car and parked behind the police car. He got out and walked up to the officers. Before he spoke, another car pulled up and the police car was completely blocked in.

"Where are you taking our friend and why?" Johnnie-Reb asked the officers.

"This is a police matter. You guys had better move on."

"Bullshit! You can bet your white ass you're not taking him anywhere unless we know where he's going and why."

Both officers began sweating profusely. They were so nervous that it was hard for me not to laugh.

"Look, it's nothing serious. We need to take him to the station to check something out."

"Okay, you drive to the station. We'll be right behind you."

Both officers were dripping with sweat and could not talk without stuttering as the cars allowed them to drive off. There was a convoy behind them. Their attitudes changed.

"Have you ever lived on the PCH?"

"I don't know what the PCH is."

"The Pacific Coast Highway."

"I'm from Detroit."

"This is just a little mix-up; we have a warrant for a man with the same name as you. His address is on the PCH though. It's just an honest mistake. We apologize. We can't let you out on the street though; it's against police policy. We'll just drive to the station and you can leave as soon as we get there. I don't think you'll have to worry about a ride back." There were six cars filled with gang members following.

"Why did you pick me up?"

"You were coming out of the apartment with a laundry bag. We thought you were a burglar."

The car pulled up in back of the police station. I got out of their car and into Johnnie-Reb's car. The two of them rushed inside taking the arm bands off.

I visited Omar one day to find a white man in the apartment. They tried to introduce me to him but I ignored them and walked straight back into the kitchen. "I need to see Evelyn Omar. Do you mind?"

"No little brother. Go right ahead." He got up and followed me. "What's up Twenty-Five? Why did you treat the man so cold?"

"A white man came to my house one day in Detroit. He was asking me about joining the police. My life has never been the same. I prefer to stay away from white people."

"Give the man a chance Twenty-Five. Give the man a chance."

"Let me put it this way Omar." I said pointing my finger at him. "I don't do business with white people."

Evelyn was standing there watching us as our voices grew louder. "Why don't you guys calm down? All of this is not necessary. Richard is alright Twenty-Five. He's a friend of mine."

Omar came close to me and whispered. "This dude Richard is going to show us how to make PCP. Me and Kojac have been looking for somebody who knows how to make the stuff for a long time. This is money Twenty-Five, big money."

I took a deep breath to calm myself before I spoke again. "Bad Karma. But, I'm a Martial Artist, not a drug dealer. That's you guy's business. From now on, I'm going to concentrate on Martial Arts. Don't get me wrong. I appreciate you guys and everything you did for me. If you need me. I got your back. I hope if I need you, you got my back. But, take a word of warning. Good does not bring about more good but, evil always brings about more evil. I think white people are evil. You guys be careful." I turned and walked out.

Johnnie-Reb spent a lot of time working out with me. I did not see Omar for a long time. Harriet could not visit because her fiancé was home. Kojac showed up at the park from time to time to play basketball or, to work out. We started regular Saturday morning games. Kojac and I were always on opposing teams. Kojac believed in winning at all cost. He would knock an opposing player down before letting him shoot. He would laugh and call the player a punk if he called a foul. Eventually the only way you could make a basket was to fight your way to the basket. The young men who came to the court could only watch until we were finished. Our game was too dangerous. Eventually, I was the only player who had not spent time in San Quentin. The guys began to call our game "Kill Ball" instead of basketball.

After the games I would stretch and meditate. Kojac always had a group of young men around him. He told them about prison life. He said that he and his friends were members of the five-hundred-pound club. The members had to be able to lift five hundred pounds of weight, otherwise, they did not consider you a man. All of the ex-cons looked like contestants in a Mr. Universe contest. I felt honored when Kojac pointed me out as the toughest man he had ever met.

Richard spent a lot of time at Omar's apartment. Soon Omar and Evelyn drove by the park to show off a new car. I suppressed my anger when Evelyn told me that Richard had helped them to get the car at an amazing discount. "I told you he was all right Twenty-Five."

They invited me to dinner. I accepted on the condition that Rihard would not be there. The lady who had worn the black negligee was there. Her name was Bobbie. I was consumed with lust for her because I could not forget the sight of her in that negligee.

Bobbie had a live-in boyfriend. He was an entertainer who did road shows and she never knew when he would show up. As Bobbie and I got to know each other she began to tell me about Herb as if she needed to release the hostility that she had developed towards him.

He had clothes stored in her closets. There was a car and an RV that belonged to him in her garage. When Herb did show up, it was to take whatever money she had.

"Why don't you get rid of him?"

"He won't go."

"Surely there are ways to get a person out of your house. You could call the police."

"You don't know Herb. He is a gangster like Kojac and those guys. He has threatened to hurt me if I call the police. I have seen him hurt people before. He means business."

"That doesn't make sense to me. No one is stupid enough to think they can control a person like that. He just does it because he knows you'll let him. Why don't you pay Omar of Kojac to ask him to leave? That is, if you really want him to go."

"They are all old friends. Herb is a member of the gang. He sometimes goes along on some of their jobs."

"Do you want me to ask him to leave?"

She laughed. "You don't know Herb. You would have to kill him or, he'll kill you."

"You don't know men. Things change when they are dealing with other men."

Omar and Kojac laughed uncontrollably when they learned that I was going to confront Herb.

"Listen little brother," Omar said. "When you go. Please come by to get a gun. Don't be a fool. You don't know Herb."

It seemed as if everyone knew Herb but me. He arrived, as everyone knew he would, the day Bobbie got a check. I came by to see Bobbie when I found out that he was there. I was sitting on the couch in the living room when Herb came in from the back of the apartment. I could see why people feared him. He looked mean and he was a really big dude. He had the muscles of a Five-Hundred Pound club member.

"Who are you?" He asked as he stormed into the living room.

"My name is Twenty-Five. I'm a friend of Bobbie's."

"Yeah Twenty-Five, I've heard about you. Listen Twenty-Five, this is my apartment and Bobbie is my woman."

I looked at Bobbie seated in a chair across from me. I was afraid that her fear of Herb would make her change her mind about speaking against him.

"I thought you told me this was your place?" I said to her.

"This is my place," she replied.

I laughed. "You're a liar Herb."

"Twenty-Five, let me talk to you in the bedroom for a minute. Man to man."

We walked into the bedroom. I went in a few steps, Herb stayed by the door and pulled up his shirt to show a pistol stuck down in his belt.

"Let me explain to you again. Bobbie is my woman and this is my place. I don't appreciate you being here. Now you see what I got in my belt. Do I have to get nasty?"

"You keep saying 'my woman.' If you were saying my wife, I could respect that. I don't know who you think you are, but I think you're a freeloader. You intimidate these women, you force your way in and, frighten them into letting you stay. You take their money and call yourself a man. I'm a man. Like I said I'm a friend of Bobbie's, not a freeloader who is out to take what she has. You don't intimidate me. Now she says she wants you to leave. She wants your clothes out of her house and your vehicles out of her garage. I suggest you do it by tomorrow morning. If you don't, I'll come back to see if you can use your gun as well as your mouth. Unless you want to try right now, I suggest you move away from that door."

Herb nervously stepped away from the door without hesitation. I walked through the living room, kissed Bobbie on the cheek and left.

The next morning, Herb and his things were gone. Omar and Kojac could not stop laughing and talking about what happened. Omar said that Herb had come by his apartment before he left." That's the bravest little nigger I ever seen in my life." Herb had told Omar.

"When he left, I told him; Herb, go and tell everyone that you encounter that you have seen the Divine one and the time is at hand." Kojac joked.

I went back to my apartment to see a woman playing football with the boys. I was excited by her beauty and her athletic ability. She could out-run, out-throw and out-catch all of the guys. I sat on the stairs watching her. She realized I was interested. I was thinking of the best way to start a conversation with her.

A tall slim figure walked into the front gate. It was Kool. He broke up the game. "We're going to need some room in the courtyard," he said. "There's going to be a fight and someone is going to get hurt. Come on out Twenty-Five."

"You think you're bad enough to call me out Kool."

"I found another teacher. Better than you. I've been training. Come on out."

Once again, I beat Kool easily. I deliberately let the fight go on longer than it should have. I wanted to show off my skills for the woman who was visiting.

Harriet, her fiancé and his two military friends came outside to watch the fight. No one had seen Harriet outside since Robert had come home. She did not look happy. I was beginning to wonder if she was being kept inside against her will.

Kool left a beaten man. The children were excited by the fight. "They could use you in the movies." One of the children said. Robert and his two friends in military clothing came up to me. "That's nothing," one of them said. "Whenever you're ready, we'll show you a real fight." I smiled and bowed. "I'm not looking for a fight."

The lady who I had been showing off for interrupted our conversation. "Excuse me," she said. "Do you have a minute?" "Pardon me, gentlemen," I said as I walked over to the lady. The three men backed away. Harriet ran into the apartment.

The lady who had attracted me was named Linda. She worked for Hughes Aircraft. She had also been a track star in school and she had a scrapbook filled with newspaper clippings about her victories. She was in the neighborhood visiting a friend. She mentioned she liked the neighborhood. She was considering moving here.

"You don't want to move into the Jungle," I told her as seriously as I could. "You have no idea what goes on around here. Take my advice, find another neighborhood."

"You live here," she smiled and said sarcastically.

Linda did not take my advice. She moved into the apartment building next to mine. She came to visit as soon as moved in. I reminded her that I thought it was a bad idea to there. I warned her to carry some type of protection. She learned what I was talking about on her first payday after she moved in. She was robbed on her way home from the bank.

I was telling her that she was lucky she got away with her life. She was angry. She did not want to admit that the Jungle was controlled by gangs. "The next time, I won't just give up my purse," she told me. "I'll make them fight for it."

"Wrong idea," I said. "These guys are ex-cons. A lot of them have been in prison most of their lives; lifting weights. You don't have a chance."

"You're the one who doesn't understand," she said. "You talk about the place, but you live here. Honest working people can't let these thugs intimidate them. You don't let them run you out, and I'm not going to let them run me out."

"Look, I'm kind of stuck here. I don't have any control over my destiny right now. You have a good job and a choice. Please get out before it's too late."

The next payday, Linda was again on her way home from the bank. A man came up to snatch her purse. She was dragged down the street until the straps broke. She had injuries to the face and the whole right side of her body where she had been dragged along the concrete. She did not look the same when I visited her. She had been tough, but she had been broken physically and mentally. She decided to move out of the jungle.

I went to Omar and Kojac to talk about finding the men who had robbed Linda. They told me they were glad I had come over. They were about to go on a mission. They needed my help. I probably would have gone along with them, but there were several ladies in the apartment. Bobbie was one of them. Omar, Kojac, and some other guys were talking about the job they were about to do. I pulled Bobbie to the side and talked to her about having sex. She agreed. I announce that Bobbie and I were about to leave. The women were giggling. Omar and Kojac were almost hysterical. "No! Twenty-five! Don't leave. We got some important business to attend to."

"I got some important business right here," I said. Bobbie and I went downstairs to her apartment. We had sex. I went to sleep. Late that night, Omar and Kojac came into Bobbie's apartment as happy as I had ever seen them. When Bobbie opened the door, they forced their way past her and into the bedroom.

"What's going on?" I asked.

"We are partying, that's what's going on. All of us are about to be rich." Omar took out some bills and threw them on the bed. "Here, Twenty-five, here's your share." "My share of what?" "And here is a little something if you feel like getting high," Kojac said before Omar could answer. He threw a Sherm wrapped in foil on the bed. "Richard has shown us how to make our own PCP. We don't them fools anymore; we're going to be rich." "The White boy?" I asked. "Yeah, we told you he was cool."

I unwrapped the Sherm; lit it, and took a hit. I think I experienced death. At first it felt like my body was being sucked away, as if it were in a vacuum cleaner. I lapsed through some kind of tunned and ended up in a field filled with beautiful green grass, flowers, and trees. The place looked as if it had never been touched by civilization.

I felt good. Better than I had ever felt before. Everywhere I turned there was beauty. I heard someone calling me from one of the trees. I walked up to it. There was a beautiful woman with long flowing hair sitting high up in the tree smiling. We just looked and smiled at each other. I felt like I never wanted to leave the place.

Then I heard another voice. This one sounded like it was crying. As the sound of the voice drew my attention, I began regaining consciousness in Bobbie's bedroom. I found myself completely nude with my hands and feet tied. Bobbie was crying; Evelyn was crying. Debra was there; Glenda was there. All the women from the apartment building, and nearly all of the women from the Jungle were there.

"What in the hell is going on!?" I yelled trying to cover myself, but finding my hand were tied behind my back. "He's alive!!" I heard a woman yell. A bunch of women came to the bed trying to kiss e. I was going crazy trying to untie myself.

After I got dressed, they explained to me that I had lost consciousness as soon as I took a puff from the Sherm. When I began speaking unintelligibly, they all felt that I may hurt someone without realizing it. The guys tied me up. Debra, Evelyn, and Bobbie called their girlfriends to find out how to bring me down off that stuff. Most of the women in the Jungle were in Bobbie's bedroom looking at my nude body. Now, I had to live with the fact that ever woman in the Jungle had seen me naked.

I still had the Sherm that Kojac had given me. I looked at it when I got to my apartment. I thought about my experience. If I had actually died and gone to another world, I sure wanted to go back. This time my only worry was, would God consider it suicide if I died of a drug overdose? Was that place Heaven? If I smoked it again, would I end up I the same place or somewhere else? I was about to light up when the phone rang.

"Hello, Mr. Brown?"

"Yes"

"This is Mrs. Carter."

"Huh?"

"The President's wife."

"The First Lady?"

"Yes, Mr. Brown. We want you to know that we are looking into your case with the Veterans Administration. Everything is going to be OK. Are you alright?"

"Yes. I'm fine, Mrs. Carter."

"Good-bye Mr. Brown."

I never had time to recover from the shock. Kojac and three other men were pounding on the door. "Twenty-five, open up man." I let them in. "That stuff must be good, "Kojac said. He was in an extremely good mood as he walked into the apartment. "I was telling these guys, if it will knock Twenty-five out, it'll knock anybody out." "Don't you think the stuff is a little too potent to put on the streets?" "Not at all, Twenty-five. The niggers are always complaining bout the stuff being too weak. They want the bomb; we'll give them the bomb." "You don't understand what happened to me when I smoked it. Don't put it on the streets, Kojac. A lot of people could get messed up with that stuff." Kojac looked around at his companions and laughed. "You can't stop us today, Twenty-five. You can't even stand up straight. That's what the niggers want; that's what they'll get. I'm putting the stuff on the streets." They walked out.

I was angry. I became angrier after I tried to move around and found out that I did not have full control of my movements. I sat down in the meditation position, feeling helpless but only for a moment. The anger took over. I put on a jogging suit and left the apartment running as fast a I could. I ran down Coliseum Boulevard to La Brea Avenue, then up the hill that seemed to go up for miles. As the sweat began to pour, I began to feel sober. After about two hours of running, I went home to shower. I dressed and went to Omar's to find Kojac.

"Where's Kojac?" I asked, walking in without knocking. Immediately, I felt the tension inside the apartment. Johnnie-Reb was with Omar. They looked as if someone had died. "I'm glad you showed up, Twenty-five," Johnnie-Reb said. "Omar is about to kill Kojac." "What's going on?" I asked. Omar answered: "Richard and Kojac

GANG MEMBER

cooked up some scheme to get ten thousand dollars from the bank. They came up with some phony ten-thousand-dollar check, and talked Evelyn into trying to cash it. They locked Evelyn inside the bank and arrested her." "Is she in jail now?" "Yes, Twenty-five and I warned Kojac before they made the deal that if Evelyn went to jail, I would kill him. I meant it." "Slow down, Omar. You are going to ruin things for yourself. Evelyn is a grown woman. She knows what she's doing. The thing for you to do now is to get her out, not get arrested yourself. Don't send yourself to prison, Omar. There are always different ways to handle things." Johnnie-Reb looked out the window to see Kojac walking up the steps. "Kojac is coming," he said excitedly. "Put the gun away, Omar," I said. "Put it away." Omar reluctantly put his gun under a newspaper on the bar. He stayed close to it.

"What's going on?" Kojac asked as he entered the apartment. Omar answered: "Evelyn is in jail, Kojac. I told you that damned check thing wouldn't work." "Don't worry, Omar. Richard is arranging for her to be released right now." "That's not the point, Kojac."

"Come on, Omar. You and me have been working together too long to fall out over something like this. I came by to tell you how much money we're making off the Sherms. We can't get them on the streets fast enough." I interrupted: "I was looking for you to talk about that Kojac. I was telling you earlier the stuff is too strong to be put on the street. It's going to kill people." "Come on, Twenty-five, did you think I wasn't listening to you? We talked about and we weakened it. I'm not out to kill anybody, Twenty-five. The stuff is selling faster than we can put it on the streets. I had to hire some more men. I ran into Kool. I let have twenty-five of them, just to help get back on his feet." "You actually gave dope to Kool? Knowing the problems, you had with him in the past?" I asked. "He came to me for help, Twenty-five. I gave him my word that I would help him. I'm trying to straighten my life out, to be less corrupt, like you, Twenty-five." We all frowned.

"I'm not going to be happy until Evelyn is home, Kojac. I suggest you look into that before anything else," Omar said. "I told you, Richard is taking care of that. Evelyn will be here in a couple of hours.

In the meantime, I want to dip some these Sherms. The workers are waiting."

Kojac took some cartons of Sherman cigarettes out of a paper bad. He carefully took a jar of PCP out of his pockets. He sat down on the floor and began to dip one end of the cigarette into the jar then the other. He would then wrap the finished product in aluminum foil. This was the way Sherms were prepared. Kojac was over anxious, the process was too slow. "Forget this," he said. He emptied some packets of Sherman cigarettes on a long piece of foil. He then took the bottle of PCP and poured it over them. "This is faster." "That won't work," Johnnie-Reb and I said it at the same time. "They have to be dipped one at a time," Johnnie-Reb said. "Do you think them stupid dope addicts will know the difference. Look at them, don't they look like they have been dipped? Come on, help me wrap these things in foil." "I'm not touching them," I said. "I got a call from the First Lady, Mrs. Carter. There is a chance the Veterans Administration is going to pay me the disability they owe me. That means I may have a chance to get out of here and lead a normal life again. I'm not doing anything that might send me to prison." "I'm not touching them, either," Johnnie-Reb said. "You're going to have every dope addict in the Jungle looking for you if you put them out like that." Kojac answered: "Look at this one, do you really think some stupid dope addict is going to recognize the difference? All they want to do is to get high."

Omar walked out of the room shaking his head. Kojac quickly wrapped a bunch of improperly processed Sherms and hurriedly got his equipment together. "I got to go and get this stuff to the pushers." He rushed out the door.

Omar was still angry. "He's lucky you were here Twenty-five. I would have killed him." "It's not worth it. Omar. "Let me give you some advice, Twenty-five. I'm just telling you this because I love you like a brother. You keep fooling around with that damned Kojac, you're going to end up dead or in prison. I'm serious, little brother." "I hear you," I said as I walked out.

The call from Mrs. Carter gave me the hope that I could still get back and regain the life that I had lost. My life in California still seemed like a bad dream. If the Veterans Administration would pay me retroactively from the time I was disabled in the Marine Corps as the law stated, I would have enough money to move back to Detroit, possibly pay off the court and, see my children.

I did strenuous workouts to fight the anxiety. I was thinking about leaving. I stopped getting high and the pain returned. I was determined to clean up my life so that I could make a new start.

Only a few days had passed when three men attacked me in the park. The men were weak drug addicts who did not have a chance. They ran off before I could ask the reason for the attack. I was attacked again by another man before I walked from the park to my apartment. This one came after me with a baseball bat. He missed a few swings and I knocked him out with a spinning heel kick. I revived him and tried to ask what was going on. He struggled to his feet and ran away.

After that fight, I walked to Kojac's apartment to find out what was happening. I found Kojac seated alone in the dark. "Come on in Twenty-Five. I figured they would send you to do the job."

"What job?"

"Don't play dumb Twenty-Five, I know they sent you to kill me just like they sent me to kill you that time." I sat down on the floor and crossed my legs.

"I didn't come here to kill nobody. I did come to ask why the drug addicts keep attacking me?"

"There is a hit out on me. I didn't know they were after you too."

"For what?"

"Those Sherms I put out on the street were no good. All of the customers want my head on a stake. I found out that Kool told everybody I deliberately tried to cheat them. He Is supposed to be with those soldier boys now. I think this maybe it Twenty-Five."

"I told you not to let Kool in on this."

"I know. I also know that I should have killed Kool a long time ago. I kept letting him get away."

I laughed "Kool is one lucky ass, Kojac. I have to admit that."

"You know what I think? I think Kool, you, me and the others have all been sentenced to die. We just keep getting the sentence delayed. I'm beginning to think there's no way out. We're all genocide victims. I can remember when all I wanted was a decent job and a normal life. If you talk to them, all the rest of the guys felt the same way at one time. We just found out that the system is stacked against us. We really don't decide who are the cops and who are the robbers. We have always been chosen to be the bad guys. The gang members. Strong men do what they have to do; we end up in prison. The weak go to work every day and get high or drunk to avoid facing the reality of their miserable lives. They'll get rid of you and me somehow. They don't have a choice. The baby boys like Kool will be all that's left of our race. Punks who have to live by the gun because they can't call themselves men without them."

"I once read an Asian proverb that said: 'A stupid man dies a stupid death.' I don't mind dying. In fact, I think I'll be glad to get out of here. I just don't want to die on their terms. If the addicts think we cheated them, we need to straighten it out. We can do that. I'll get whatever cash I got; you do the same. We'll walk through the Jungle tonight. We will locate as many customers as we can. We will tell them that somehow a bad product got on the streets. We'll tell them that we are ready to refund any of the money or replace the product. If we reach enough of them, the word will spread on the streets. Them Special Forces guys are a different story. They have been wanting a fight since they got here. I say we find them before they find us."

"You know Twenty-Five, you changed my whole outlook." Kojac leaped to his feet. "Tonight, we handle all unfinished business." Kojac hesitated for a moment. "Before we leave the building, I need to holler at my apartment manager. I believe he' been screwing my wife. I want to handle this before we leave."

Kojac and I walked out of his apartment and headed for the manager's apartment. Kojac knocked, the manager opened the door. It sounded like a party inside. There was loud music and the smell of marijuana. Seeing Kojac he came outside and closed the door behind him. The size of this man was amazing. He made Kojac look small.

"I left you a message to get in touch with me earlier. What the hell happened, why are you coming just now?"

"Let me give you one of them San Quentin pep talks. I told you not to come to my house leaving any messages. You stay away from Debra. That is not my girlfriend. She is my wife!" Kojac turned to walk away. The man lunged forward to grab Kojac's shoulder. Anticipating an attack, Kojac turned, blocked the man's arm, grabbed it and broke it with his knee. The man screamed in pain, tried to throw a punch with the other arm. Kojac took the other arm and broke it over his knee. He then took the bigger man, lifted him over his head, walked to the edge of the balcony and threw the man from the second floor to the courtyard.

"I've been wanting to do that for a long time Twenty-Five. Let's go."

We spent most of the night paying off PCP users. It did not take long for the word to spread around the Jungle that we were offering refunds for the bad dope. It was close to dawn when we went to Harriet's apartment. Harriet smiled when she saw me and Kojac at the door. Her fiancé was there without his friends. Harriet invited us in. Her fiancé looked around nervously as if he were looking for a weapon.

"Don't get excited man. We didn't come here for a fight."

"I don't know." He replied. "I see you brought your boy."

"Not to fight you. I heard you guys bought some bad Sherm. It came from us. We want to make it right by refunding your money or replacing the dope when we restock. How do you want to handle it?"

"Kool told us that you guys deliberately put bad dope on the streets. He said you tried to force him to sell the stuff. He was telling us how he threw the stuff back in your faces."

"Kool has been here?"

"Yes!" Harriet said excitedly. "You should have seen how he performed. Telling us how he threw the dope in you guy's faces."

"Do you know where he is now?"

"He's helping Robert's friends look for you two."

"Let's go Kojac."

"Wait!" Robert called out. "I don't have any way to contact my friends to let them know to stand down."

"Don't worry," I said." fighting us won't be like fighting women."

Harriet smiled. Her fiancé dropped his head in shame.

We were on our way back to Kojac's apartment when the soldiers showed up. Kool was standing back waiting to watch the fight. Both men were good strong fighters but, they were no match for the strength Kojac had acquired during his years in San Quentin and my years of training under Grand Master Shim.

Realizing they could not win, the men pulled concealed weapons. One of the men fired. A bullet grazed Kojac's arm. I did a forward roll and ducked as the other soldier fired and missed. Kool threw one of the men an Uzi. He fired into the air.

"All you have to do is breath too loudly," the soldier said. "I'll put more holes in you than Swiss cheese. You guys didn't really think you could beat Special Forces, did you?"

There was no way Kojac or I could get to the men in time. Kojac and I looked at each other.

"What do you think Twenty-Five?"

"I say we take it to the dirt Kojac. I'm so tired of California, I don't know what to do." Kojac and I both smiled.

"See you on the other side Twenty-Five." We nodded and got ready to charge the guns.

Suddenly there was gunfire like we were in a war zone. There were a lot of men surrounding us and firing into the air. The soldiers turned to see Omar and ten other gang members. All of them had guns aimed at the soldiers.

The soldiers dropped their weapons; raised their hands and backed away. When they felt they were at a safe distance, they turned and ran away. Kool had already taken off running in another direction.

"Where is Kool?" Kojac asked.

GANG MEMBER

"There he goes, running between those two buildings," Someone answered.

"I'm going to kill him!" Kojac exclaimed. Running towards Kool.

"No. I'm going to kill him." I said running along with Kojac. As I was running, the words began o echo in my head, "I'll kill him. I'll kill him. I'll kill him."

I stopped running. I had flashes of Kool sitting with me and Mary smoking weed. Then in my dark apartment eating stolen bread and smoking weed. Suddenly, all of my strength left. I did not want to fight anymore. I just wanted to go home.

I walked back to where Omar and the rest of the gang were. It was not long before Kojac joined us. Kool was used to running and hiding. He always got away. Something, someone up there must be looking out for him I thought.

"I got some news for you Twenty-Five." Omar said. "Somebody named Dee Dee called. She said that she was your sister-in-law. She said she wanted to tell you where you can locate your wife."

It was hard for me to contain my excitement. For the first time there was the feeling that things were finally turning around. Omar and I started walking towards his apartment. Kojac joined us. Kojac addressed Omar.

"I'm going to need to pick up some more stuff to replace the dope I need and to get the business rolling again."

"I don't know where the stuff is Kojac. You and Richard were responsible for hiding it."

"It wasn't me and Richard. It was you and Richard."

"You're wrong Kojac. Richard said you and him were going to put it in a safe place."

"Where is Richard?"

"Omar, I know you're not going to tell me you lost eight gallons of shit. We're talking about big money now, millions."

"We'd better talk to Blue. He knows what's going on. He'd better."

We were near my apartment so I said good-bye and walked away from the group. Kojac and Omar continued their conversation as I walked away. Later Kojac came to my apartment.

"It's fucked up Twenty-Five. It's fucked up."

"What do you mean?"

"Richard showed us how to make PCP. Embalming fluid is one of the main ingredients. We had got hold of eight gallons of the stuff. Now no one knows where it is."

"Embalming fluid? Is that the stuff I smoked that night when I ended up naked with all those women in the room?"

"That's what it was. Now no one knows where the eight gallons went. I had to give Omar one of those San Quentin pep talks. I told him from now on, I want mine off the top."

"What are you going to do?"

"I still got dope to replace. I've got to do something but, I'm going to give you a little advice Twenty-Five. If you don't stay away from that damned Omar, you're going to end up dead or in prison."

A cold shiver ran down my spine as I recalled Omar saying the exact same words about Kojac.

Kojac did not have the funds to make another buy. He decided to do an early morning robbery to raise funds. He robbed a McDonalds on Crenshaw Blvd. The police got to the scene before he could get away. There was a long shoot out. The SWAT was called. Kojac's car was so badly damaged by bullets that it was unrecognizable. The only other vehicle on the street was a garbage truck. Kojac made his to the garbage truck. He shot the driver, took the truck, and made his getaway. Kojac's shot up car made the morning news.

Mary was working in downtown Los Angeles. She had a job at the Transamerica building. I called and arranged a lunch date for the next day. I got some rest and cleaned myself up. Somehow, I was beginning to think I was coming out of the nightmare that I thought would never end.

I felt like my old self as I left my apartment headed for the bus stop. Kojac was on his way to see me as I was leaving. We stopped to talk in the middle of Coliseum Blvd. Neither of paid any attention to the passing traffic. "Twenty-five, come on and go with me; I need your help with something." "I can't do it, Kojac. I just heard from my old lady; I'm going to meet her right now."

I could not help but notice that one of Kojac's forearms looked as if it had been hit by buck shots. "What happened to your arms?" I asked him. "Oh, this is nothing. I was just doing a little work and got bruised. Look Twenty-five, I just contacted some friends in Las Vegas. They got a sweet deal going down there. Me and you could fit right in; we'll be rich in no time. Together, we could take over." "Can't do it, Kojac. I'm still hoping I can get back to working a nine to five, paying my bills, and playing with my children on the weekends." "What are you going to do, Twenty-five?" "First, I'm going to find out if my wife is all right, then I'm going to get myself off dope, and go back home to Alabama." "Back to Alabama, huh?" Kojac smiled. "When you get to Alabama, you tell them, the time is at hand." We hugged, then walked off in different directions

There was something magical about my bus ride into downtown Los Angeles. It was like I was seeing L.A. for the first time. In some ways I felt like my old self, but deep inside I knew I was just not the same person. Because of my experiences in the Jungle, I knew firsthand what it means to be born again.

CHAPTER FIVE

The Birth of Crack

The number of pretty girls working in the Transamerica building was amazing. Whoever did the hiring was a person after my own heart. Mary looked right at home. She had changed as well. She had studied to get her GED and had plans to go to college.

"Twenty-five, always thought that you would find me and save me," she said after we hugged. "I found out that I couldn't even save myself."

Mary had taken an extra hour for lunch, so we had a long friendly talk. The fact that she was doing well took away my feelings of guilt. I always worried that, if anything happened to her, it would be my fault for bringing her to Los Angeles.

On my way back to the Jungle, I felt good. I even felt like the punishment for my sins was complete. If my monthly veterans' compensation was enough for me to live on, I would have time to go back to school to work on a degree. I was also interested in finding another Grand Master to continue my training in marital arts. I still had classes going on in the park. However, I wanted to be a real master of marital arts and for that, I needed more training.

My use of PCP decreased after my out-of-body experience. I still found myself wanting to get high in order to deal with my physical pain. I began using mostly marijuana. Linda came by my apartment some nights, and some nights I spent at Bobbie's. No matter where I was, I had developed the habit of jogging early in the mornings. I was returning from a run one morning when I noticed the SWAT team moving in Omar's apartment building.

I rushed over to Bobbie's to call Omar. I told him to get rid of his dope. The police were in the building. I took a bag of weed I had in Bobbie's bedroom and flushed it down the toilet. "What are you doing?" Bobbie asked. "I'm getting rid of my weed. The Police are searching the building. I think it's a drug bust." We looked outside.

The SWAT team was not concerned with the rest of the building, only Omar's apartment. Everyone came out to watch as they brought Omar out. They laid him face down on the concrete in the courtyard. "Twenty-five!" He was yelling. I walked closer until the policemen pointed the guns at me and motioned me away. "Look after Marie for me." One of the policemen kicked his head into the concrete. Omar raised up again, his face bloody. "Look after Marie for me, Twenty-five."

After they took Omar away, I went back to Bobbie's. "That's a whole lot of fire power for a drug bust," I said. Several ladies from the building had gathered at Bobbie's to talk about the police activity. "That was no drug bust," someone said. Bobbie had everyone laughing about me flushing my weed down the toilet for nothing. "No, this was about that funeral home robbery," someone else said. "Didn't you hear about it on the news?" "What funeral home robbery? How come I don't know anything about this?" I asked. "Because you were getting high and having sex with Bobbie. That was the night you passed out and we all saw that body of yours." "Why rob a funeral home? They don't have a lot of money on hand, do they?" "Embalming fluid, Twenty-five. Eight gallons of embalming fluid was taken. They make PCP from embalming fluid. You're so dumb."

Blue came down to tell me he was moving from the Jungle. He said that things were not going well and he needed to get away while the getting was good. He warned me to do the same.

"I don't know what happened to the eight gallons of embalming fluid, Twenty-five. I really don't know, but I know it's time to get out of the Jungle, you know what I mean?"

"Eight gallons is a lot of stuff to hide. I'm willing to be the White boy set up Omar and Kojac, and I'm glad that I'm not involved."

"Me too, Twenty-five." He reached out to shake my hand. As we walked away in different directions, Blue turned and called out to me. "You know, Twenty-five, I sure thought you were the police." We both laughed.

The receipt of the Veterans Administrations decision finally came. The findings were a disappointment. I was rated thirty percent disabled. I had anticipated the lowest possible rating. My monthly compensation was on hundred-thirty-three dollars a month. They also ruled that compensation would not be paid from the time I became disabled in the Marine Corps. Instead, I would be paid from the time I stopped working for Chrysler. I did not get enough money to pay my back rent or to continue renting an apartment.

I would have to find other means of support. I knew I had to get off drugs first. Since my attempts to clean myself up were unsuccessful, I went to the Veterans Administration Hospital's Mental Hygiene Clinic for drug rehabilitation.

The Jungle changed after Omar and Kojac left. Evelyn tried to sell drugs for a while. Twice she called me to come over when someone came into the apartment with a gun. The second time I went to her rescue, the man had an Uzi. I managed to wrestle the gun away from the man. Then I tried to convince Evelyn that selling dope was not a good idea. Omar could handle it. I could not sell dope, and she should not sell it, because I could not provide security. Eventually, Evelyn gave up her career as the drug queen of the Jungle.

Kojac had become a legend. Several people had a fear that he would return to the Jungle to kill them. His wife, Debra came to me and offered to pay me to act as her bodyguard. I assured her that Kojac had no intention of doing her any harm. She disagreed. Debra began to visit me quite often. She always had drugs and we got high together.

I realized that I would have to move away from the Jungle to cure my addiction.

After Omar's drug business stopped, younger men took over the sale of Sherm in the Jungle. The alley behind Omar's apartment became known as "Sherm Alley." The alley was set up so that people could drive through to buy drugs just like a fast-food restaurant. Fist fights gave way to shootings and because of the activity in the Jungle, the police began driving through the alley with a show of force. Nearly every night there was a shooting incident. What seemed like dozens of police cars would speed through the alley with lights and sirens. This cleared the alley of buyers and pushers for a while, but they would return after the police left.

Finally, an iron gate was placed at each end of the alley. After that, those who drove through would run into a dead end. Drug buyers would park near the entrance to the alley then walk through to purchase the dope.

Eventually, a new drug appeared on the scene. The drug users called it "rock cocaine." It seemed the drug of choice for a lot of PCP users. The sale of Sherm and angel dust decreased as more users turned to the rock. Rocks usually came in two sizes, twenty-five-dollar rocks and fifty-dollar rocks. This was far more expensive that the ten-dollar Sherm or a ten-dollar bag of angel dust. The most peculiar thing about the rock was, it always made the user crave for more. The cravings were unending. Once a person began smoking it, they were willing to sell everything they had to get more.

Poor people usually could not afford to buy the twenty-five or fifty-dollar rocks, so they began asking the pushers to break off a "crack.' The "crack" was a little piece of the twenty-five-dollar rock, and the little pieces could be sold for a dollar or more. Since most of those arrested for using rock cocaine were poor, they were arrested for cracks instead of the rock. It was the police who began using the name "Crack" for rock cocaine.

I was first introduced to the drug when Johnnie-Reb and I attended a party. It was amazing how women loved the drug. Once they got hooked, women would do anything to obtain crack, including any sex act. Pushers took advantage.

Crack was a powerful drug. It was easy to spot a user because each user would begin selling everything, they had to obtain the drug. You could see peoples' televisions leaving the house. Furniture, jewelry, and things people had worked years to obtain, all sold to the drug pusher or to obtain money to buy the drug.

Crack would change whole neighborhoods. My heart sank as I saw single mothers being evicted along with their children. People who were otherwise honest would suddenly become creatures who would steal from or sell their own parents for crack. Some women would offer their children for crack. If someone was intentionally trying to destroy a generation, they had succeeded.

The pushers became younger, the users grew older. Older women, who had earned the respect of children would now offer their bodies to those same children for crack. Children, watching the adults throw their lives away on crack, eventually lost all respect for their elders. The crack dealer ruled the streets. Children turned to gangs to find what they could longer get at home. Otherwise, nice neighborhood would completely change to gang territory in a matter of days.

I had begun using crack after being introduced to it at the party. Because I could maintain self-control in using the drug, several women enjoyed getting high with me. The women told me that I was different when using the drug because most men became uncontrollably paranoid, they could not fight the urge to get more after the dope was gone, and I never came up with any weird sexual request.

I did have a certain level of control, but I also experienced the urges. I did not like crack because to me, it's the closest thing to demonic possession I had ever seen. No crack user-controlled crack. Like an evil spirit, crack had a mind of its own. Once you got hooked, the drug was in control. No matter how much you loved a person or no matter how much they loved you, once they were on crack, they could no longer be trusted.

GANG MEMBER

Part of the goal of martial arts training is "being master of your own impulses." After I began feeling the loss of control, I stopped using the drug. Later, I checked myself into the Brentwood Veterans Administrations mental hospital to get myself completely off drugs.

Although I was hospitalized, the Veterans Administration still refused to raise my disability payments. I had no income to afford a place to live if I left the hospital. While I was still in the hospital, I managed to get a job at the Veterans Administration Regional Office in Los Angeles. My job as a file clerk did not pay enough to afford an apartment.

Larry Davis and Jack Vance were other veterans who worked as clerks. Since our positions were so low, it was astounding how the other workers looked down on us. We were almost forced to stick together because the other Black men who had better pay positions would not speak to us at all. It was a weird place to work.

Larry had a room in a cheap hotel across from MacArthur Park, near downtown L.A. After I was released from the hospital, Larry helped me to get a room in the hotel. Our paychecks were barely enough to cover the rent. I was lucky in that I had the VA compensation to help me survive. The place was roach-and rat-infested, but it was all we could afford. I always ended up lending Larry and Jack some of my compensation check so that we could eat. After work, I would go up on the roof to practice martial arts. Larry was interested in learning, so I began teaching him.

Jack lived in a cheap hotel in another part of L.A. When they went up on his rent, he moved to the same place as me and Larry. The three of us practiced every night. As part of our training, we began running around the lake in MacArthur Park. As time passed, my stamina grew.

At first, we ran around the lake once a day, then twice. I kept increasing the number of times I made it around until Larry and Jack would stop and sit on benches waiting for me to finish. After a while, they began to go to the hotel, shower, and then come back to see me complete my run. Eventually, they told me it was useless trying to run with me. I got to where I could run around the lake twenty-seven times. Since Jack had a steady girlfriend and Larry had several, I felt that I owned my stamina to me not having sex. Larry was popular everywhere. He introduced me to several ladies who lived in the hotel. None them suited my taste.

My moving into the place created problems for Larry from the beginning. We were all due at work at eight o'clock each morning. I was glad to have the job, and I was determined to be on time. Larry, Jack, and I caught the bus on Wilshire Blvd near the hotel. The Supervisor knew we lived at the same place, yet I was always on time.

After Jack moved in, we caught the bus together, and the both of us were always on time. Larry had been arriving late since he first got the job. His excuse had been the bus did not run that early. The supervisor did not like the fact that he had been played. He began to show a dislike for Larry and treated him with disrespect.

As Larry became better at marital arts, his confidence grew. He wanted to use his skills on the supervisor. I advised him against it. Larry was disappointed with his life. He seemed to become more disappointed after I was introduced to his cousin Sheryl. Sheryl was a very special lady. She looked like a beauty queen. She owned a business that provided bus transportation for trips to Las Vegas; she bought new cars every year, and when she was younger, she had won several beauty contests. One contest had earned her the title, "Miss Compton."

Sheryl would drop by from time to time to check on her cousin. After Larry introduced us, he told me about her accomplishments and about the type of men she liked. I told him how special I thought she was and I wanted to go out with her. Larry assured me that Sheryl would never agree to gout with men in our condition. We had the lowest paying jobs and lived in that rat-infested place. Her dates were always rich guys who drove expensive cars. Larry was amazed when Sheryl invited me to dinner at her stylish apartment. He was shocked to find that I spent the night. Soon I was driving Sheryl's new car. I also accompanied her on trips to Las Vegas.

Since she already had a fabulous apartment, Larry became furious when a relative gave Sheryl a house. After that, his whole conversation was about how his family treated him differently. "Here I am staying in this roach and rat-infested hotel, and they give her a fucking house. It's not fair. No one ever did anything for me," he complained. Larry's anger grew daily. When the supervisor confronted him again about being late, Larry cursed him out and walked off the job. He decided he could live off his martial arts skills.

While Jack and I kept our jobs, Larry's new profession became snatching purses. We could not talk him into coming back to work. After all, he now had more money than Jack and me, and he did not work. He met a girl named Linda after she had seen him make a daring robbery, and escape an exciting police pursuit. Linda was a pretty girl who had facial scars to show that she had led a rough life. She had done time in jail. After they met, she moved in with Larry, and they worked together stealing and robbing. Later, Larry met a White prostitute called Popcorn. She needed a pimp, and Larry decided to take the job.

Sheryl informed us about a job opening with the Southern California Rapid Transit District. I applied for the job. Jack did not feel confident to try driving the big buses and Larry was very happy being a pimp.

Sheryl's information came at the right time President Carter was out of office, and President Reagan was making a lot of changes. Before, Federal Employees never had to worry about being laid off. Because of President Reagan's changes, new employees found themselves being laid off. I was one of them. There was a lot of rumors about how they would find a way to keep the Whites employed, and they did.

Driving the bus was the job of my dreams. Women liked the uniform, and I came home each day with a pocket filled with phone numbers. As long as there were no problems on the job, I never had to worry about supervision. I got a chance to see how beautiful California was and I made good money. Before long, I had moved out of the hotel. I found a place in West Los Angeles with a swimming pool, tennis court and gym. I was living better now than I had in Detroit.

I visited Larry in the hospital after Sheryl informed me that he had been stabbed. Larry told me that his girlfriend Linda, had stabbed him after she became jealous over some of his other whores. The doctor said he was lucky to be alive because the knife wound was less than a quarter-inch from his heart.

I visited the hotel to talk to Linda, who gave me the more believable story. She said, that Larry had become obsessed with using the martial arts that I had taught him. He had kicked her in face and had broken her jaw on two separate occasions. She had warned him that if he ever kicked her again, she would get him while he slept. After his last attack, she waited until he was asleep, then stabbed him in his chest. She said Larry woke up and chased her for nearly ten blocks with the knife still in his chest.

Linda, Popcorn, and Larry were still together the last time I visited him at the hotel. He also had four other girls and two big transvestites in the room. I felt that it was time for me to stay away. The next thing I heard about Larry was that he had used martial arts to kill a man in MacArthur Park and was sent to prison.

When I went to the Jungle to visit Evelyn, the Jungle had changed and Evelyn had changed as well. The Jungle was now filled with people from Belize. I found it strange meeting Black people with accents I was not familiar with. Several families from that country had moved into Omar's old apartment building. Evelyn had become a close friend of a lady named Frances. Frances was a devout Christian. She had converted Evelyn. Both of them went to church every Sunday and Bible study on Wednesdays. All thoughts of dealing drugs or being a drug queen had vanished. Evelyn's conversations now revolved around the Bible. Frances would accompany Evelyn on her visits to see Omar. They would hold prayer sessions for him. Occasionally, I got to talk to him on the phone. I apologized for not coming to see him. I explained to him that I could not force myself to go near a prison. My brief experience being incarcerated still gave me nightmares. "I understand, little brother." Omar would say.

Frances was married to an Army veteran. She had an eighteen-year-old daughter, Shawn, who was pregnant. Shawn, was half-White. Frances had previously been married to a White Army Officer.

She had divorced him because he became impotent. Frances shared that she experienced a lot of racial problems during the marriage. On one occasion, she had overheard a White officer's wife complain about the seating arrangements at a dinner they had been invited to attend. "I know you're not going to seat me next to the nigger," the White woman had said. The man's impotence and accumulation of racial incidents had caused the marriage to break up.

Things were not going well with her second marriage either. Life with a black man was far too different than the life she had been accustomed to. He found it hard to keep a job after his discharge from the Army and it was obvious that she was out of place in the Jungle.

I felt like she was special. I had actually experienced losing my breath when I first saw her. Her face glowed and her body was indescribable. Our mutual attraction was hard to ignore. I tried hard not to stare at her whenever we were together at Evelyn's.

Evelyn asked me why I did not meet her husband, get together with him and go out on the town. I explained that, I did not want to know her husband or to associate with him in any way. I liked his wife too much. I told Evelyn how special I thought she was and given the chance, she would be mine.

Shawn came to visit Evelyn every time I came over. Evelyn told me that she was attracted to me. I let her know that I could never bring myself to go with an eighteen-year-old. Legal age or no. Being as strong in the Christian faith as she was, Evelyn was shocked to find out that Frances admitted that she was attracted to me. The only communication that she had with her husband was arguments. She went to church. He drank.

I told Evelyn that the reason the man constantly argued with her was because he knew she was way out of his class and there was nothing he could do about it. The arguments grew worse. Frances would sometimes come over crying about something stupid her husband had said. Before long he left home and did not return. After the separation, Frances and I began to talk. Like her husband, I knew that she was out of my league as well.

Just walking down, the street in a pair of shorts caused men to stumble over things looking back at her. Some fell off bikes and drivers had accidents. Evelyn always returned with stories about their adventures.

"You, my boy," Evelyn would say." should bottle whatever you have. I keep telling you. Along with all the women in the Jungle, you got mother and daughter liking you.

Frances told me that she would never again date a man who did not go to church. I began accompanying her to church. I knew that going to church would not be enough. She needed someone she could look up to and respect, someone who had made something out of their life and, had stability. She did inspire me to improve myself.

I enrolled in West Los Angeles College. I studied Computer Science. I was happy beyond belief when I made an A in class. I also began working as an extra in movies. I got a chance to audition for the movie *The Last Dragon*. However, I was so excited that I got stage fright during my audition. I did get a chance to meet Smokey Robinson and Barry Gordy. I was pleased with the progress I had made with Frances' inspiration.

CHAPTER SIX

The Black Knight

I purchased a beautiful motorcycle and a black helmet that had other bus drivers calling me "Darth Vader." Frances took a job at some factory near downtown Los Angeles. After a while she moved out of the Jungle into a very nice apartment in West Covina.

On one of my visits, she was very sad to tell me that the White man who owned the factory had asked her to marry him. I was surprised at how sad she seemed. She said that she had accepted his proposal because he was very rich. I understood. I told her that I could not blame her for wanting financial security. I had learned that there was too much control over the lives of Black men. We never knew what would happen from one day to the next. I remembered how my life had changed in one day after I had been called to court.

One lesson that I had learned was that poverty should be avoided at all cost. As a Black man in America, I knew that I could end up sleeping in the park at any time. I was happy to have spent time with someone as special as her and I had learned not to cling to anyone or anything. I was sincerely happy for her.

The little extra work that I was doing in the movies was exciting. I enjoyed speeding around on my motorcycle from one set to the next. I met James Earl Jones and Rae Dawn Chong on the set of a movie called *City Limits*. I actually bumped into Deby Boone on the set of a movie called *Sins of the Past*. When Richard Pryor was making *Brewster's Millions*, I was actually a team captain for the casting agency. I could sigh up extras.

By this time, I was in church a lot less without Frances and at the strip clubs a lot more. I had gained the same popularity with the dancers in Los Angeles as I had in Detroit. The thing about strip clubs was, every time you think you've met the world's most beautiful woman, you end up meeting someone more beautiful. In addition, there was always something exciting happening in the clubs. I can never forget the night a stripper asked for my motorcycle helmet and did a show with it that had the audience going wild. I wanted to frame the helmet so that I could always remember the dance.

Another night, I sat right in front of the stage hypnotized by the performances. The women seemed to be dancing for me because they had my full attention. One man became so angry that he jumped up and yelled. "What the fuck is going on here. Are all of these bitches dancing just for him? Aren't they supposed to be dancing for everybody?" The girls, the customers, and the bouncers were cracking up as he was escorted from the bar. I never felt so proud.

On another night, I was wearing a short leather jacket when a big guy seated at the table next to mine suddenly said. "Give me that coat." I looked around at him and smiled thinking he was joking.

"I said, give me that coat!" The man repeated.

I looked at the man again and saw that he was serious. I turned my attention to the dancer on the stage.

"You think you're going to get out of here with that coat but you're not."

At that point, I removed my jacket and laid it across my legs. When I did, the man made a leap and tried to grab it. My anger overwhelmed me and I began beating the man unmercifully. Before the bouncer could pull me off, I had thrown him onto the stage and was banging his head against the floor.

None of the girls made me forget about Frances until, I met Vanessa Nathan. When I first saw her, I lost my breath and my mind went blank for a moment. I could think of no one who could match her face, her body or the way she danced. Vanessa had the physical control of a Yoga master. It was easy to talk to her because she was from Detroit. She drove a Cadilac Seville.

She was looking to be a movie star and, she was excited that I could sign her to be an extra in Richard Pryor's movie. She was impressed by me being a team captain for the casting agency. We spent a lot of time talking about being in the movie together. I was to pick her up on the morning that we were due on the set. I had not planned to go to the bar that night but, I wanted to see her dance.

When I entered the bar, one of the dancers approached me to ask if I had heard about Vanessa. "Heard what?" I asked.

"She's dead."

I laughed. "Vanessa's not dead, I just saw her last night."

"It happened late last night." The dancer said. "She was in this place that got robbed. The robbers did not want to leave any witnesses so they blew everyone away with a shotgun, including Vanessa."

After I found out that the story was true and, learned that Vanessa's death had something to do with crack, I remained sick for days. I missed out on the filming of *Brewster's Millions* and, eventually quit the bus company. All I wanted to do was to go back home to Alabama.

The only thing that kept me from leaving Los Angeles right away was that the death rate surrounding crack was phenomenal. One did not need to be a user to end up getting killed. All you had to do was to be around it.

Again, I though about my wife, Mary. Again, I felt guilty about bringing her to such a place. I knew that Mary loved to get high and that she loved cocaine. If everyone was using crack, more than likely Mary was too. Before I left, I had to find her, and if she was on the drug, I had to get her away from it.

I had Mary's address on Ninety-first Street. I had been through the neighborhood a year before. It was a nice clean neighborhood with neat apartments. Things had changed. After dark, most of the people who drove down the street were looking for crack.

The street was becoming overcrowded with pushers. As one man drove slowly by waiting for a pusher to appear he found himself being rushed by young men on both sides of his car. Both of the men were trying to sell their crack. The two men began arguing about who would make the sale. The driver got nervous and drove farther up the street to another pusher. The young men continued arguing.

"Hey man, you guys work for Roy. That's our end of the block down there. You don't have no business rushing our customers."

"Y'all can't tell nobody where to sell dope. Hell. The streets belong to everybody."

"Oh yeah? You just wait. We'll see about that."

The young man walked off motioning to his coworkers to follow. The men went into the apartment of a woman in her early thirties. She did not have the appearance of a drug dealer. However, she was one of the biggest dealers in the neighborhood.

"Yeah Lila," the young man said after they got inside. "The same thing Is happening. We have to tell them every night to stay on their end of the block. Every night they do the same thing. They keep stealing our customers."

Lila got up and walked over to her closet. "Don't worry. If talk don't help, I got something that will." She began pulling weapons out of the closet and passing them to the men.

"Take these. Go back out there and back them up. Make sure they understand if anyone of them crosses the center of this block again, that's their ass."

The young men took the weapons and went back out on the street. They formed a line and walked up the block like a police riot squad. One of the men fired a shot into the air. The other pushers began to run.

"That's right. Run mother-fuckers and remember, from now on, you bastards stay on that end. Anybody who crosses the middle of this block selling dope is a dead man."

GANG MEMBER

Roy was the dealer on the front end of the block. His workers ran to his apartment to tell him about the incident. Roy began pacing the floor. "Okay, that's the way they want to play it huh? Well, you guys don't worry, we'll just close down for the night. Tomorrow, it will be a different story. I promise you; you'll never have to run again."

After that, most of the pushers were armed. There were frequent shoot-outs and a lot of young men died. The street was smoky, as if there had been a gunfight as I slowly rode my motorcycle looking for Mary's apartment. I was amazed at how the place had changed. I kept motioning the men away who came running up to my bike to sell crack. I could not find the place. I decided to call her the next day to get the correct address.

Mary's apartment was between Roy and Lila's apartments. When I returned the next night, I heard a lot of fumbling around when I knocked on the door.

"Who is it?"

"It's Twenty-five." I answered.

"Go to the back door."

I walked around the building to the back door and knocked again.

"Who is it?"

"It's Twenty-Five."

A really big nervous guy jerked opened the door holding a pistol. "What do you want?"

"Is this Mary's apartment?"

"Speak up nigger!" The man yelled, pointing the gun close to my face. "What do you want?"

I quickly twisted the gun from his hand and kicked him over the kitchen table. Another man came running into the kitchen from the front of the house pulling a pistol from his belt. I had taken the other man's gun and was already aiming at his head.

"I wouldn't do that." I said smiling and shaking my head.

The man dropped the gun, raised his hands and backed up against the wall. Another man rushed into the room. He saw me and stopped. "Brother-in-law!" He yelled. "Calm down you fools. It's my brother-in-law, Twenty-Five."

The man was Mary's brother, J.T. He yelled to Mary. "Hey sis, you'll never guess who's here. It's Twenty-Five."

Mary was in her bedroom getting high with J.T. and a man named Easy. When J.T. introduced me as Mary's husband, the man excused himself and said that he was going home. When I asked what was happening, I learned that Mary was indeed a heavy crack user. She still worked for the insurance company and supported the habit by allowing Easy and his brother deal crack from her apartment.

Easy's brother was preparing the stuff on the stove in the kitchen. J.T. was pushing the dope on the street. He sometimes worked for Lila.

In Detroit, J.T. had been a well-known Martial Artist and player. It was hard for me to understand how he had ended up in Los Angeles with a crack habit and working for young punks to support his habit. Easy had said that he had to go home, but I sensed he and Mary lived together and he had made the statement for my benefit. I was right.

I began visiting often. My plan was to protect Mary; gain her confidence by smoking crack with her and then, suggest that we quit together. On my visits, I got to know Easy. He was another ex-con who always bragged about the time he spent in San Quentin. He tried to act tough, however, it was easy to tell he was nowhere near as tough as Omar, Kojac or, any of the gang members in the Jungle.

Like Frances's husband, he knew Mary was way out of his league. He had heard about me and had been impressed by the stories Mary and J.T. had told. Nearly all of his conversations were about prison life. Easy, Mary, J.T. and I spent hours smoking crack.

Easy made money selling dope then would smoke everything he made. The pushers liked Mary and respected her as much as a crack addict could be respected. As they got to know me, they would ask me behind Easy's back. "Why don't you take her out of here man. She doesn't belong here."

I did not get to talk to Mary alone much but, when I did, I threw out hints about giving up crack. She seemed to be in agreement.

However, I knew that there was no way to quit in this atmosphere. She said that she was waiting for a Knight in shinning armor to come and save her.

I stopped by one night to find J.T. had been so badly beaten that he was unrecognizable. He had been selling dope for Lila and had smoked up the money that he was supposed to turn in. It was said, the only reason he was not killed was because he was Mary's brother.

Another time, he had smoked the crack which he was supposed to sell but, had substituted a piece of white soap to sell to the buyer. The man had returned with a shot-gun; broke down the door and came into the apartment looking for him. The man threatened to kill everyone in the house. Vanessa's fate came to my mind. If I was beginning to think that helping Mary was a lost cause, I changed my mind. Also, it was a sad experience seeing a fellow Martial Artist end up this way.

With my frequent visits, Easy began asking me if I wanted to join him in dealing crack. He said that with the money we were wasting smoking, we could easily become rich. He had tried to convince Mary but, she liked to smoke too much. I told him that my religion would not allow me to sell dope to another human being. I could deal with hurting myself but, causing harm to another human was bad Karma.

Easy had a sister who came by to purchase dope. He did not like the fact that his sister liked me after we had been introduced. She began coming by looking for me. I now had an excuse to visit more. There was a drastic change in the atmosphere when Easy and I were in the kitchen talking. Several of the young pushers gathered on the back porch. Unaware that Easy and I were in the kitchen and could hear their conversation. One of the men spoke.

"Easy ain't shit man."

"I know man. I just wish Twenty-Five would take Mary and get her the fuck out of here."

"That nigger Easy don't even have a place to stay. He keeps his sorry ass in Mary's apartment bragging about San Quentin to make people think he's tough."

"I'll bet he was someone's bitch in San Quentin." The men laughed.

"Let's go outside." I suggested. Easy's feelings were really hurt.

"No, Twenty-Five. Let them niggers talk. I don't give a fuck. I'll remember."

From that time on, Easy was uneasy every time I came over. He did try hard to hold on to some money from the dope he sold. He drove by to pick me up one day in a Cadilac, as if he were trying to impress me. When I inquired about the car, he said a woman offered to let him keep the car for fifty dollars' worth of crack. He was about to return the car and collect the money. I would follow him on my bike to give him a ride home.

When we got to the woman's apartment, her husband was there angry about what she had done. When the woman paid Easy the money, the man walked out of the house telling Easy that he was going to blow his head off as soon as he walked outside. The fear on Easy's face made me laugh. He was really afraid to leave the woman's apartment.

"Let's go." I pleaded.

"I ain't going out there, that fool is out there with a shot-gun."

"What are you going to do? Stay here for good?"

"You can leave if you want to Twenty-Five. I ain't no fool."

I grabbed my helmet and walked outside. The man was standing there with a shot-gun. I looked at him and smiled as I walked to my bike. I could tell that the man did not want to hurt anyone. He was angry and hurt over what his wife had done but, he was not ready to go to prison. I got on my bike and rode to the door blowing the horn. The man got into a truck and left. "Come on Easy." I yelled. "It's safe."

Easy peeked around the door sweating and trembling. The next time I visited, Easy was in the hospital. He had been shot. The story was, Easy had gone out to a car to sell a rock when a man shot him; took his money and the dope he was carrying. Some of the workers recognized the man as a rival gang member.

While Easy was in the hospital, the gang drove to the shooter's neighborhood and located his house. They got out of their cars and began firing into the house. Before they finished, they nearly brought the entire house to the ground.

The two-day hospital stay gave me the opportunity to talk to Mary. I never mentioned us getting back together. I did preach about giving up crack and starting a new life. On the day that Easy came home, he was furious that Mary did not come to pick him up from the hospital. He was afraid to confront me. He calmly talked about how he had been shot. He was uncomfortable about my being there even though his sister was with me. I listened for a while then went home.

When I got home, my phone was ringing. Lila was on the other end. "Listen Twenty-Five, I have a message from Mary. That nigger Easy is tripping out. She said that after you left, he played Russian Roulette with her. She's about to leave and she wants to know if it's okay for her to stay with you for a while."

"Shure. But she doesn't know where I live."

"Don't worry. She'll find you."

Mary knew that I lived in West Los Angeles, but she had left without the address. I worried that she would not be able to find my place. There was little chance of her finding my apartment with just luck. I was wrong. I went walking. After I had walked for blocks and blocks, I saw her walking towards me.

I notified an old buddy that I may be having problems with Easy and his gang. Jack came over to watch my back. I expected gunplay from Easy and the gang but, when Jack saw him driving by my apartment, he was alone. The guys did not want to help him. For two nights in a row, Easy drove by and kept going. On the third night, Jack drove up next to him, looked him in the eyes and laughed. Easy sped off. After that, I began driving down Ninety-first street on my bike.

Easy was walking towards the street when I made my second trip through the neighborhood. He spotted me and ran to the apartment to get his brother. I parked my bike, took off my helmet and walked to meet the two of them walking towards me really fast at first, expecting their gang members to follow. They slowed down after looking around to see the other men were staying back.

There was the sound of tires burning rubber as Jack's car jumped the curb and stopped beside Easy and his brother as they pulled their weapons. Jack pointed his Uzi at them.

"Twenty-Five don't believe in guns. I do. You can drop them pistols and play with him or, keep them and play with me. How do you want it?"

Both guns fell to the ground. Easy began backing away. His brother met me and attempted to throw a punch. I blocked the punch and began to throw punishing kicks and punches with the gang watching and yelling with excitement. He fell to the ground unconscious. Easy turned and ran. I never saw him again. However, it was not long before I heard that he had been killed in a gang related shooting.

Kicking the crack habit was not going to be easy for Mary. I truly had no problem quitting because, having kept myself in shape for Martial Arts most of my life, I actually felt guilty each time I smoked. I was actually more addicted to Martial Arts than any drug. I hated the fact that crack had a mind of its own and took over a person's life. All of an addict's money went to crack. I loved nice apartments, clothes and cars more. If I was going to waste my money, those were the things I would buy.

I told Mary that my plan was for us to move back to Alabama. However, I would never go anywhere near my mother with a drug habit. My philosophy was, exercise could cure anything if you kept working out so hard that the only thing that you could do was to fall asleep. Mary and I began running up the big hill on La Brea Avenue every day; practicing Martial Arts and going for long walks.

Mary was really skinny when she moved in with me but, a few runs up that hill brought her shapely legs in no time. We both agreed that being away from the drug scene made it easier to quit. Unfortunately, the cravings for crack can remain with you for years even after you quit. If you have a weak mind you're hooked for life. I was glad that I had experienced the drug for myself. That way no one could ever talk or trick me into using it.

GANG MEMBER

My plan for a gradual withdrawal abruptly ended when Mary had a seizure one night. Her heart stopped beating and her breathing stopped. I don't know how long I spent doing CPR, pounding on her chest and praying to GOD that if he would let her live that I would never use crack again or let her use it again.

When Mary came back around, she did not realize what had happened. She viciously attacked me when she learned that I had flushed the remaining crack that we had down the toilet. It took a long time to convince her that she had actually died. She was finally convinced when I told her after what happened to her, I would never go near crack again and, if she did, we would have to separate for good.

We both quit without any problems. Sometimes it was hard to even stop dreaming about the drug. To me, being addicted to crack was no different than being demon possessed. Mary and I had never agreed to get back together or to stay together but, months passed and we both worked out very hard every day. Mary regained her stripper's body and I began to feel like my old self again. I began looking for a Martial Arts school and began training under Grand Master He Il Cho.

Mary began taking Hapkido; got a job at a bank in Beverly Hills and our lives began to normalize. Grand Master Cho eventually allowed me to teach my own class as Grand Master Shim had done. After a while I talked Mary into joining Grand Master Cho's class. Mary earned her black belt.

I told Grand Master Cho about my plan to move to Alabama to open my own school. He advised me on how to proceed. It was after Grand Master Cho left Los Angeles and moved the World Headquarters of the Action International Martial Arts Association to Albuquerque, New Mexico. It was in 1998, that we finally moved to Alabama.

During the years I was away, I ran up big telephone bills calling my mother weekly and having long conversations with her. She loved old Tarzan movies. I recorded a lot of them, planning to watch them with her. Before I made it home, my mother began telling me that she was worried because she was losing her memory. Later we learned that she had Alzheimer. Mary and I dropped everything and made the move to Alabama. My mother could not recognize some of the people that she knew when I got home; but I was blessed that she always recognized me. I was terribly upset about her illness and the fact that we never got the watch the movies that I had recorded. After a while she got to the point that she did not know anyone and her condition deteriorated to the point where she had to be placed in a nursing home.

For me, it would be hard to describe Alabama without using the word evil. It was never a surprise when people from all over the world speak of the evil there. It was also never a surprise when someone would ask me where I was from and finding out that, when I answered; "Alabama." The response was; "Oh yeah, I went through Alabama one time. I got out of there as fast as I could."

Nothing about the place could describe how it really was. Mary and I had arranged to rent a house there from Los Angeles. When we arrived, some white men were in the process of cleaning the carpet. When we told them that we would leave and return after they finished, we could hear the remark. "That's good enough for them." They left with the job being incomplete.

There were only a few black people in the neighborhood. Some of the white people were friendly, others would turn their heads to avoid looking or speaking. In some businesses whites went out of their way to show the hatred for blacks. Just like in Jim Crow days and before, some whites would ignore a black person to wait on another white person first or, deliberately do something to make you wait.

In one instance, a woman continued to recounting pennies that she kept removing from a cash register. On weekends, we visited my sister in Birmingham. My brother-in-law rented a booth in a flea market where they sold goods they had bought on discounts. On one of our visits, a white family noticed that children's bikes at my brother-in-law's place were considerably lower than the other vendors at the same location.

"Hey." The lady remarked. "These bikes are five dollars cheaper and they are the same as the others."

"Yeah, but you would be buying black." Was the remark.

In a conversation with a repairman who came to the house, we learned that interracial marriage was illegal in the State of Alabama. The man was upset because he was married to a white woman. Mary was amazed. I felt like I had gone back in time.

I contacted the Board of Education in an effort to teach Tae Kwon Do classes with the school system. The people that I talked to did not know or, pretended not to know what Tae Kwon Do was.

Some blacks were no better. I presented my credentials to Alabama State University, a historical black school, and applied to teach a Continuing Education Program. "Oh, I guess you're the master?" The man said sarcastically.

"No, I'm not a master however, I do have instructor certification from one of the world's greatest Grand Masters."

The disappointing thing about Alabama State University was that the man promised to arrange the class and when I arrived to teach, he had not done so.

I started teaching classes at Houston Hill Community Center, Grace Christian Academy and then Floyd's Community Center. I never got enough students to help my mother financially, so eventually I got a job as a security guard.

As soon as I began to work, an old nightmare came back to haunt me. It had been thirty years but the State of Michigan issued wage withholding documents for my salary. The same case that caused me to be locked up and to lose my job all those years ago was reopened. They were still trying to collect child support for Antoine. The irony was, Antoine was not my child; I had never been allowed a DNA test and Antoine was now under court order to pay child support himself.

This time I was writing President Clinton to have the case investigated. The courts began the same threats that had ruined our lives in 1976. Along with President Clinton, I wrote the Department of Justice, The FBI, The Department of Health and Human Services, The Family Independence Agency the Alabama State Bar and, the NAACP. Eventually I found out that nearly all lawyers avoided child support cases. I had even saved a letter from Johnnie Cochran's office turning down the case and advising me to seek another attorney. I realized that there was no way that I could convince anyone that the court had acted improperly.

I began focusing on the facts that: Minnie was married to another man when she became pregnant with Antoine; she gave the child my name instead of his biological fathers'; we had not seen each other in five years when she got pregnant; I was also incarcerated and lost my job for no reason.

After I continued to write President Clinton, he asked Congressman Terry Everette to investigate the case. After Congressman Everette began looking into the case, the court found that while I was working for Chrysler, all of my salary had been taken because they had been collecting for two cases. I was voluntarily having deductions for my children. The additional payments the court ordered for Minnie consumed my whole check.

After Congressman Everette's request for an investigation, Detroit's Friend of the Court protected itself by dismissing the case. The court could not come up with a reason for incarcerating me without allowing me to have a DNA test. They changed Minnie's child support case to an alimony case then began trying to collect twenty-five thousand dollars in alimony. Again, I began writing the President asking how I could owe alimony to another man's wife.

I thought about the information I had received from a man named Rudy in a strip club thirty years ago. Eventually, I took a chance and paid someone to look through old records to find the marriage license for Minnie and a man named Rudy. GOD was with me again. I was sent a Wayne County Marriage License for Minnie L. Brown and Rudolph Eady. The two of them had been married on September 28, 1970, State file number 70971.

I also managed to get a letter from the third Judicial Circuit Court of Michigan, dated January 9, 2001 stating my Judgment for Divorce from Minnie, "had specific language which shows no alimony was to be paid by either party." The court was not willing to admit any wrong doing after I provided Congressman Terry Everette with a copy of Minnie and Rudy's marriage license and the letter showing I was never ordered the twenty-five thousand dollars the court was trying to collect. The court changed the case once again from an alimony case to a child support case.

I was summoned to court once again for the same child support case that I had been incarcerated for, knowing that the only reason was to give the false impression that the court had acted properly. Unlike the time when I was incarcerated, I got to court with a copy of Minnie's marriage license and another request for a DNA test.

"We are not going to give you a DNA test for a thirty-year-old case." The Friend of the Court representative said. I argued that I had a right to the test. The man talked Minnie into dropping the case. He threatened that I would end up in jail again if I did not leave the case alone. I notified the Michigan State Bar, The Alabama State Bar and Congressman Terry Everett. I produced a letter sent by Congressman Everette dated January 30. 2001 that read

Dear Mr. Brown:

Thank you for letting me know about your efforts to clear up and alleged debt which the child support enforcement authorities are collecting. You sent a copy of a letter from the Michigan Family Independence Agency, dated July 21, 2002, that clearly said you do not owe child support, and that child support case (number19666-044693DM) was paid in full and is closed.

You also sent a copy of a letter from the Third Judicial Circuit of Michigan, dated January 9, 2001, which States that your judgment of Divorce "has specific language which shows no alimony was to be paid by either party." Nonetheless, the court thought you had a child support debt due, and they said they are scheduling a hearing.

I appreciate this opportunity to be of assistance to you in this matter. I have shared your letter with officials at the US Department of Health and Human Services, and have asked them to give you every cooperation and consideration in settling this. I have also asked if they can suggest a lawyer who will represent you in the hearing.

I will write to let you know as soon as I receive any response to my inquiries on your behalf. In the meantime, if you have any further questions or information you need to give me, please talk with Mrs. Victoria Ebell in my Washington office. For details on legislation and other useful information, I invite you to visit my website at http//www,house.gov/Everett/. With best wishes"

The letter was signed. "Terry Evertt."

The Michigan State bar referred me to an attorney who would represent me for the money that had been unlawfully taken and for being wrongfully incarcerated. The attorney had me to believe that he was working on the case when he was not. After several months he sent a letter asking me to remove his name from my fax distribution list. I never got my money that had been taken by the court or any restitution for my illegal incarceration, the loss of my Job, or the inhuman harassment that covered a thirty-year period.

I was sure that divine intervention could help to resolve the problems I had with the court. I began going to church. Mary would go sometimes but, she held on to her belief that most people who went to church were hypocrites. We both joined the Dexter Avenue King Memorial Baptist Church. Reverend Michael Fox Thurman was the Pastor. We became good friends. I began attending bible study classes and gained a new respect for the Christian religion in discussions with other who attended the classes. Dr. Martin Luther King had once been the pastor of the church and I had always held an interest in the place after an experience I had there during the civil rights movement. Reverend Thurman eventually began studying tae kwon do with me.

Mary and I were happy to finally be free of the harassment and for the chance to start over. I continued teaching tae kwon do classes at the community centers, and participated in summer programs with the children. The house we had rented went up for sale. We were given an opportunity to purchase it, and I was excited about owning a home.

Overdue student loans prevented us from being able to use my Veteran's Certificate of Eligibility to purchase the home. We also became victims of predatory lending. We had been approved for the loan on the home when the lenders raised the interest rate twice before we closed the deal. The normal rate during that time was around three percent. We were told that, because of past-due student loans, our rate would be sixteen percent for one year; then we could refinance at the normal rate. Mary was angry and did not want to close the deal. I convinced her that Black people did not get fair treatment in the South and that we were lucky to get the house at any rate. I told her that the year would pass quickly, and soon we could own the home with a normal interest rate.

The predatory lender was Associates. After the year was up, Mary was looking forward to getting the rate reduced. Associates informed us that the company had been sold to CitiFinancial Mortgage and this company would not honor Associates promises to reduce the interest rate. Before we could see other means to refinance the house, the Department of Education took my twenty-five-hundred-dollar student loan, added eight thousand dollars interest, then began taking my disability check. We found ourselves with more bills than we could handle. When I made an attempt to stop the deductions from my disability check because I was disabled, the reply was, I was not disabled by the Department of Education standards.

CHAPTER SEVEN

The New Name For Niggers

In November 2003, Mary and I were hired by the United States Postal Service as "casual employees." The Postal Service hired temporary workers for the Christmas holidays. My tae kwon do classes at the community centers did not pay enough for us to cover our bills and "casual employment" sounded like what I was looking for. I could work part time and continue teaching my classes.

Everyone was nice when we went to orientation. We were assigned our jobs and shifts. We were told at the time we would be treated with dignity and respect. Mary and I did not get the same shit because my employment was held up when I presented my discharge papers from the U.S. Marine Corps showing I was a disabled veteran. I presented my Medical Board Report from the Marine Corps, and convinced the people in Human Resources that my disabilities would not prevent me from doing "casual" work. After my employment was approved, there were no more positions on the shit that Mary had been assigned.

The supervisor for my shift came in to give a speech during orientation. He was a big Black man with a loud voice. His attitude came across as arrogant and disrespectful. He talked about what he would and would not tolerate o his shift. He seemed to be trying to scare us and no one in the group wanted to work under his supervision. Those who had worked for the postal service before told the rest of us that this was a supervisor no one wanted to work for. He was always rude, he always used foul language, and it was hard to find a more unpleasant person.

I did not feel that I would have any problems, because I was willing to follow the rules and to do a good job. Others warned my that they would rather give up the job than to work under his supervision. The Human Resources representatives made excuses for his behavior. "He may be a little rough" they would say, "But he loves his job and the job is very important to him." A woman named Judy and I were assigned to his shift.

I found the term "casual employment" to be terribly misleading after I got on the job. I was thinking I would have time to keep up my tae kwon do classes while working part time for the Postal Service. After being hired, I came to find out the casual employees on this job were required to work six days per week and up to twelve hours a day. Casual employees did not get any holidays off and had no employee rights or benefits. The supervisors had adopted a program of pushing the casual employees as hard as possible to get as much work out of them as they could. Since the casual employees worked for less than half the pay the career employees made, the supervisors, bragged about big bonuses the received for pushing them. I soon learned that in reality, "casual employment" was an experiment in slave labor conducted by this particular branch of the United States Postal Service.

Work at the main post office in Montgomery, Alabama was like taking a trip into the past. In reality, one could see what it was like during slavery. My supervisor played the role of a slave who had been promoted to overseer. His actions gave the impression that, the more abusive he was to Blacks, the more acceptable he was to Whites. I personally felt that he was a reincarnated slave. He was especially abusive to Blacks and the abuse was extreme when any White person was present. The majority of the "casual employees" were Black. The only reason they accepted the job and the treatment was they could not find other work; they did not know what they were getting into or they felt if they accepted the abuse long enough, they could one day get career employment.

His White counterpart was not as abusive, but the two of them seemed to be competing to see who could be more disrespectful. The two of them constantly yelled, cursed and threatened to fire he "casuals," as they called them. Although the White man did not really like the Black one, the two of them sometimes go together and boasted about their abusive treatment of the casuals.

My supervisor had a White girlfriend who also worked for the Postal Service. His attitude changed when he was with her. He seemed to enjoy showing her off; disrespecting Black women and proclaiming that he would not have a Black woman. When she was not around, all his sexual advances were to Black women.

I made friends with a lady named Jn. She had arthritis and was visibly in pain after working a few hours. We began talking, when she noticed me limping badly like her. We both began the workdays okay, but before the twelve hours were up, we were both limping badly. I became upset after I noticed ty supervisor seemed to actually enjoy the woman's pain. The more she limped about, the more he yelled and cursed at her to move faster and work harder. He would walk behind her and laugh at her pain.

In most cases, he would deny a casual employee's request for time off. He did have his favorites, usually women who did not reject his sexual advances or complain about his abuse and disrespect. Jen eventually quit because she was in too pain to come to work one day, and she if she called in sick she would be fired.

I became popular after the word got around that I was involved in martial arts and I was the author of a book. Soon, guys would talk to me about martial arts and women would talk about my book. The supervisor disapproved of my popularity. It was inconceivable to him that any Black man could be respected unless it was him, a supervisor for the U.S. Postal Service. To him and the others who profited from getting as much work done by the "casuals" as they, "casual" was the new name for nigger.

Some career employees had developed a dislike for "casuals" because "casuals" prevented them from getting overtime hours. "Casuals" were forced to work on any and all f the jobs that the career employees did. The career employees could leave after their eight-hour shifts, and if any of their work was left undone, "casuals" were required to finish the job. We were informed that we could not leave until all of the work was finished. In most cases, were sent to complete two or three different jobs before we could leave. "Casuals" had to be more qualified than career employees, who were only required to do the job they had been hired to do.

For several months, Mary and I saw each other only in passing because we were on different shits and had different days off. At the end of our temporary appointment, we were both rehired because we both did our jobs well.

After learning that we were married, a Korean supervisor suggested that we be given the same day off. My supervisor vehemently disapproved. It was amusing to him to keep us apart from each other. After we were given the same days off, he usually found some way to switch my day. Neither he or the White supervisor showed any disrespect to Mary; for they did not know how I would react. The White supervisor would often remark that he would not want a man with my skills working for him.

Judy held a job at Baptist Hospital and worked as a casual employee for the Postal Service. Judy and I became friends and got close enough to give each other a hug whenever we met. My supervisor liked Judy a lot. His attraction for her was obvious. It also became obvious that he did not like me or any other male anywhere near her. The other employees often made jokes about his obsession with keeping us away from each other. On several occasions, loud argument occurred when some of the career employees stated conversations with Judy. The career employees could argue because they had employment rights. "Casuals" could be fired immediately if they talked back. As time passed, Judy began to complain that my supervisor was constantly threatening her to keep other guys away from her.

I did not like the job, but Mary was happy that I was working and I was determined to keep the job at all cost. Ther supervisor would make jokes about my pain. As he had done with Jen, he made an effort to place me on jobs that he considered hard and when I overheard him telling another employee that he would break me, I was more than ever determine to stick it out. Once again it was like I was in the Marine Corps, being ordered to function while in severe pain. I became determined to keep the job.

Veterans working for the postal service informed me of my ability to take the postal exam for career employment. They told me as a career employee, the salary more than doubled, you had benefits, two days off instead of one, eight-hour days instead of twelve and union representation. As a Service-Connected Disabled Veteran, there was no downside to me applying for career employment.

I visited Human Resources to learn that although no postal exams were being given at the time, by law, a Service-Connected Disabled Veteran could open an exam at any time. The Human Resources representative, however, had learned about my teaching martial arts and participating in marital arts activities. After finding that I was receiving a disability check, it was decided that I was lying to the government about my disability. The lady was angry that I was doing martial arts and getting a check, and she decided to deny my right to open an exam. I was given a paper advising me of the law, then told the law was no longer in effect.

When on of the supervisors asked Mary and I to bring our tae kwon do uniforms to work so we could take pictures for the postal newspaper, I had the feeling that the real reason for the pictures was to prove that I was collecting a disability check illegally.

The longer I worked for the Postal Service, the more I learned about my supervisor and some of the other supervisors. Since the casual positions were held by people who could not find other work and casual employees could be fired at any time, sexual harassment was common. The career employees began to tell stories about numerous cases that had been brought against my supervisor and the way the office covered them up.

He began to hit on Judy. When Judy rejected his advances, he punished her by choosing the hardest jobs for her. I asked her why she did not report him; she said she had a child and needed both jobs. I was pushing a cart of mail one night when I spoke to Judy as I passed. The supervisor threw a tantrum. "Brown!" he yelled. "What in the fuck are you doing, we need the damn mail. Bring the fucking mail on down here. You don't have no fucking time to talk!"

I wanted to confront him, but I knew I would be fired on the spot, and I could not disappoint my wife. On the other hand, I could not let the matter go because I knew that once it got stated, the abusive language would only get worse. My pain would cause me to get irritated enough to hit the supervisor and I would end up in jail.

I looked over the papers we had been given when we were hired. The Post Office's promise was that employees would be treated with "dignity and respect" was a joke. When I told some of the other employees that the treatment was actually in writing, signed by the supervisor, they did not believe it.

I wrote to the plant manager about the post office's promise to treat employees with dignity and respect, and about the supervisor's constant yelling and cursing. My complaint was sent to the person who had been standing right there when the supervisor had done the cursing, and I realized my writing had been in vain.

I was called into this person's office, and told that my supervisor was an Ex-Marine who had been a drill sergeant and that he had brought this drill sergeant mannerisms to the job. I told the gentleman that I had been a Marine also, and any Marine would consider my supervisor a disgrace to the Marine Corps. Drill sergeants used the abusive language when training Marine recruits. However, they did not continue when the training period was over. In addition, no one in their right mine would want to go on a job where they were treated as if they were going through Marine Corps boot camp.

I became more popular after it was learned that I had reported the supervisor. Some of the career employees told me about his rise to power. I was told that an extreme racist once held the position of supervisor. They said the woman was extremely obese; constantly ate doughnuts, and rarely left her office. When my supervisor was hired, he befriended the woman by belittling Blacks. He would gladly volunteer to do the woman's dirty work when it came time reprimand or fire Blacks. In return for his service, the woman helped him get the supervisory position.

The man I had reported my supervisor to was said to have been hired after him and was later promoted over him. On several occasions, Whites were promoted to positions that my supervisor felt he should have gotten. He told us that he had been told by a Marine Corps officer that he would always be at a disadvantage because of his skin color. It was obvious that he hated black skin and considered his skin the reason for his problems. Belittling Black would prove to the Whites that he was different. Once, when a machine brown down and a White mechanic was sent to repair it, he told the White man, "These machines act just like niggers."

I arrived at work one day to find out that he had launched a vicious verbal attack on a young lady who worked as a casual employee. He had driven the girl to tears. Everyone's conversation that day was about this shameful verbal attack on the young lady.

His sexual advances to Judy had also increased. Judy said that her spirit had been broken when, after rejecting one of his advances, she had been ordered to work alone on a machine for twelve hours in an isolated part of the plant for several days. I knew that Alabama was probably the only place these incidents could be allowed to go on without anything being done. I wanted to see what my supervisor would do if he had to face a man without the protection of the U.S. Postal Service.

I printed up flyers inviting him to fight three rounds as part of a marital arts demonstration. I was careful not to threaten him. I handed a flyer to the White supervisor in order to let him know the offer was for him also. I put some on the bulletin boards and in the break rooms so everyone in the post office was aware that the challenge had been made.

As the employees learned about the challenge, people began to shake my hand, thinking me for standing up to what they considered to be a monster. When asked if he was going fight, my supervisor said, "No." The men and women began to tease him. He even became quiet for nearly a week. Then he began sending me to other supervisors to work. He told them that I was a good worker, but he did not like my attitude.

As soon as I began working for the postal service, I informed my supervisor that I needed a few days off in July so that I could visit Grand Master Cho in Honolulu and test for my second-degree Black Belt. My supervisor's response was, "We'll work something out." When the time came, my request was denied.

I had never taken a day off, so I called in sick in order to make the trip. I was so worn out by the six-day, twelve-hour work weeks, I was barely able to perform. I told Mary that I did not feel that I was ready at that time. However, she encouraged me to take the trip anyway. I was in such bad shape when I arrived, I put on my worst performance ever. When I told Grand Master Cho about the job, de did no believe it was possible to make a person work six days a week, twelve hours a day without holidays. "This is the United States." Grand Master Cho said. "They can't do that." Everyone that I talked about the job found it hard to believe.

When the postal exams eventually opened, I took several tests for career positions with the Post Office. I passed all of the exams. The Black and White supervisors were okay with the way they could keep Mary and I separated with the long hours and six-day schedule. The continued to rehire me for "casual" appointments, however they were determined that I was not going to get a career position.

There was an opening for the position of "rural carrier." A rural carrier delivered mail from a truck and there was very little walking. The job was perfect for me, and I had passed the exam to qualify me for the position. After I had passed the drug test and all the other requirements for the job, I received a letter to report to a doctor in Georgia for a physical exam. The other veterans wondered why I was sent three hundred miles for a physical when no one else had been.

The postal service's letter ordered me to report for the physical on June 8, 2004. On June 11, 2004, I reported for work. My supervisor's supervisor instead of George White met me at the time clock and asked me to the office. Once there, he informed me that the orthopedic surgeon who examined me reported that I was unable to stand or walk for over four hours a day.

He said because of the doctor's report, I was terminated from the casual position; denied the position of Rural Carrier and I could not be used in the other positions which I tested and passed. I was asked to turn in my badge and to leave immediately.

I was relieved to leave the post office. I had never been in a place where there was so much evil. Other veterans told me that it was not right to wait until after I passed the exam to terminate me and as a service-connected disabled veteran, the law prevented me from being terminated because of my disability.

I filed a discrimination complaint with the Equal Employment Opportunity Commission. Although I was not a career employee, the union representative helped me through the process and represented me during the mediation session. During mediation, he asked the higher supervisor why I had not been offered "reasonable accommodations." "Well, Mr. Brown should have asked for reasonable accommodations." Came the reply. That was the first time that I had heard about reasonable accommodations. Later, lawyers for the postal service would fraudulently report that my case had been sent to the reasonable accommodations committee before I was terminated.

After I lost the job, I began noticing changes in Mary that led me to believe that she was having an affair and had started using drugs again. She would work six days a week and disappear on her off days. She began hanging out with a group of young partying people at the post office.

GANG MEMBER

On our thirtieth anniversary. Mary and her new friends took a trip to Detroit. I was not invited. Mary's sister had been telling her about a new drug, "Ecstasy." It was some type of pill. I never bothered to learn about the drug. I did ask Mary if she had started using again. She said no but I could tell that she was not telling the truth.

After I confronted her about never being at home, she got angry and moved in with her friends. Once again, I could not blame her for leaving. Our marriage seemed to amount to one hard time after another. Mary continued to work for the postal service as a casual employee, I kept telling her that the twelve hour, six-day schedule was not healthy but, she seemed to be satisfied with her new life, whatever it was. She was careful not to let me know where she lived but I had no desire to look for her. I just hoped that things were better for her. I assumed that they were because she would sometimes come by the house to pick up items to be used for parties.

With no job, no wife and the Department of Education taking part of my disability check. I got behind on the mortgage, lights, gas, and water. The utilities were soon shut off and I found myself in the same position that I was in Los Angeles. I was informed that there were laws protecting veterans who would lose jobs because of service-connected disabilities. I was advised to report to the Department of Veterans Affairs. Just like when I was discharged form the Marine Corps, the Department of Veterans Affairs sent me to another doctor who would state that I was okay.

When I explained to the doctor that I had just been terminated because of disability, I could see that the doctor found it amusing that I had been denied work because of disability then, denied disability compensation because the doctor said that I could work. Some information about my condition was deliberately omitted by the doctor. There was no denying that this was a racist con game with members of the government agencies watching each other's backs just like gang members. The only difference was, gang members were more honest.

The game had not changed since the Viet Nam Era and had possible gone on since blacks had been serving in the military. Seeing the doctor laugh after realizing the determination meant that I had no means of support made it hard for me to control my anger however; I thought about the poor black veteran who thought that he could change things by bringing a gun into the Veterans Administration Office and ending up with a prison sentence instead of his benefits.

I realized that one of the strategies of the white racist was to eliminate legal means of survival and to invest in prisons. This would keep the American Slave Trade in effect. There had to be some realization the without legal means of survival, crime was all that was left.

I began writing the President, Senate, and Congress again inquiring as to how they expected service-connected disabled veterans to survive if work is denied because of disability and compensation is denied. I wanted to know if it was okay for a veteran to lose his ability to earn a living because he had been disabled while serving the country.

In examining my records, I found that several facts had been altered in order to justify the denial of disability compensation. I also found out that, while serving in the Marine Corps, my evaluations had always been good until the decision had been made to discharge me for "Physical Disability."

I began to understand the Tijuana jail incident. While waiting to be discharged, I went to Tijuana with two other Marines. We were given overnight passes however; we were arrested after we got drunk. We notified the Marine Corps that we had been locked up in Tijuana but never got a reply. We were aware that the Mexican government may not have relayed our message.

The Tijuana jail was like being in another world. The cells were overcrowded. We were placed in a cell reserved for Americans. There were four beds and twelve people in the cells. The only available water was in the toilet in the center of the cell. The water in the toilet was the only available drinking water unless you had money. You could pay the guards for drinking water. If you could pay, the water was delivered in dirty, empty milk cartons.

The food consisted of some kind of soup that looked like sewer water. The soup contained fish heads with the eyes still intact. At night, we were given bread. The bread was all I ate for twelve days. I went broke buying drinking water. After I ran out of money, I traded my watch, ring and belt for the water.

Some of the men drank from the toilet. The guards would take the prisoners possessions. In one incident, a guard asked to see a watch that belonged to one of the prisoners. The man was reluctant to hand the watch through the bars but, the guard insisted that he only wanted to see it and promised to give it back. When the man handed him the watch, the guard walked away. Some of the Americans would send for money that would be taken by the guards.

There was a women's cell on the floor below us. There were a lot of foreign women locked up there. At night some of the guards would go into the cells, tape newspaper over the bars and rape the women. You could hear the screams during the night.

After the twelve days, I decided to break out. When the cell was opened for some of the men to be released, I walked out with the group, I managed to run through the door when they realized that I was not included in the group to be released. I threw several guards around and made my way to the streets. I ran through the streets of Mexico not knowing where I was going. I did make my way to the United States Border Patrol. After a long discussion with me explaining that I was a member of the United States Marine Corps, the men apologized and informed me that they had to maintain a good relationship with the Mexican Government and that they could not aid an escaped prisoner. They did however promise to notify the Marine Corps that three Marines had been locked up there. They took me back to jail.

It was not long after the Border Patrols report that a Marine Corps Officer came to arrange for our release. He asked that the Mexican officials not file charges for my escape. I was told that they knew I was there but decided to teach me a lesson by leaving me there. Looking back, I can see that the real reason for leaving me in jail was to have me listed as a deserter. Had I not broken out, I may have been charged with desertion.

There were some angry Marines after they learned that I had broken out of jail in another country only to be returned by my own government. The Marine Corps decided to hold a summary court martial for my being AWOL in order to have something negative on my record. The officer who served as judge in my case was a hard and mean Marine. He actually considered me a hero for my escape. He considered my situation a joke. He placed me on probation.

The Marine Corps would still use the incident to place something negative on my record. On my DD214, they underlined: "One period lost time on current enlistment." No reason was given for the lost time. Like the Marine Corps, the U.S. Postal Service would use deception to avoid the payment of disability compensation. Instead of reporting that I had been terminated after they sent me for a medical exam, the report said that my employment had ended because my appointment had ended. The Department of Veterans Affairs ignored the medical report and used the falsified report to deny compensation.

Although I was upset about the way my marriage had ended. I did understand Mary's feeling that the government would continue to block any means of my being able to support myself or a family. After thinking the situation through, I began to realize that we had actually broken up a long time ago in Los Angeles. It was my fault that I found her to rescue her from crack. Maybe she did not want to be rescued in the first place.

I entered a rehabilitation program with Alabama State Rehab. I spent a year going through some computer training and a micromanagement program to help me learn about running my own business. I felt rather uncivilized living without lights, gas and a phone, but I did realize that I had lived through worse. With the knowledge that the only reason for my problems was the government's refusal to abide by their own laws, I continued to write government agencies for help.

I was about to complete the rehab program when the sheriff came to put me out of the house and place my belongings on the street. This time I did not have to become a gang member to survive. Completion of the rehab program made me eligible for a grant to open my own business and I was able to rent a building to open a Martial Arts Studio.

At the age of fifty-eight, I entered the Tae Kwon Do competition at the Alabama State Sports Festival. I won first place and gold medals for sparring, forms and creative forms. With the help of the grant from Alabama State Rehab. I opened Percy Brown's Institute of Cho's Tae Kwon Do in Montgomery Alabama.

When I'm alone, I think about Mary and the adventures we shared. I also think about the guys that I shared the most exciting time of my life with. I never say Kojac again. He ended up on death row. The last thing I heard about him was that he tried to hang himself twice. I visited Omar after he was released from prison. His hair had grayed a little, but he looked well. The last time I saw Blue, he was still surrounded with beautiful girls. I heard that Johnnie-Reb had gotten married and someone said that had seen Kool in jail.

I heard that Mary had remarried. No matter what happened between us, I sincerely hope that she is happy. I try to think of the good times we shared, but I can't avoid thinking about my last conversation with Omar. His last words to me were, "Twenty-five wherever you go in the world, we will always be brothers and you can always depend on me to have your back. But I have to be honest with you, I don't trust your wife."

It may be that things would have been different if I had been able to support myself and may family. But as I look back, I can't think of anything more valuable than the education I gained from hard times. I don't get hung up on material things – they can be taken too easily. I don't put my faith in humans – they can be disappointing. When I die, I want to go back to the place I visited when I overdosed on drugs. My belief is that a clear conscience is the only way. I have been convinced that every thought and act is rewarded, good or evil.

www.ingramcontent.com/pod-product-compliance
Lightning Source LLC
LaVergne TN
LVHW061528070526
838199LV00009B/411